THE FIRST STEPS IN ALGEBRA

AF655816

G. A. WENTWORTH, A.M.

HAWK PRESS

Published by

Hawk Press
4836/24, Ansari Road, Daryaganj
New Delhi – 110 002
Phones : 9643330713, + 91-11-23278618, + 91-11-35676207
E-mail : thehawkpress@gmail.com
www.thehawkpress.com

Copyright © 2024, Editor
ISBN : 978-93-93971-78-4
All rights reserved.

No part of this book may be reproduced, stored in a retrieval system, transmitted or utilised in any form or by any means, electronic, mechanical, photocopying, recording or otherwise, without the prior permission of the copyright owner. Application for such permission should be addressed to the publisher.

PREFACE.

THIS book is written for pupils in the upper grades of grammar schools and the lower grades of high schools. The introduction of the simple elements of Algebra into these grades will, it is thought, so stimulate the mental activity of the pupils, that they will make considerable progress in Algebra without detriment to their progress in Arithmetic, even if no more time is allowed for the two studies than is usually given to Arithmetic alone.

The great danger in preparing an Algebra for very young pupils is that the author, in endeavoring to smooth the path of the learner, will sacrifice much of the educational value of the study. To avoid this real and serious danger, and at the same time to gain the required simplicity, great care has been given to the explanations of the fundamental operations and rules, the arrangement of topics, the model solutions of examples, and the making of easy examples for the pupils to solve.

Nearly all the examples throughout the book are new, and made expressly for beginners.

The first chapter clears the way for quite a full treatment of simple integral equations with one unknown number. In the first two chapters only *positive* numbers are involved, and the learner is led to see the practical advantages of Algebra in its most interesting applications before he faces the difficulties of negative numbers.

The third chapter contains a simple explanation of negative numbers. The recognition of the facts that the real nature of subtraction is counting backwards, and that the real nature of multiplication is forming the product from the multiplicand precisely as the multiplier is formed from unity, makes an easy road to the laws of addition and subtraction of algebraic numbers, and to the law of signs in multiplication and division. All the principles and rules of this chapter are illustrated and enforced by numerous examples involving *simple* algebraic expressions only.

The ordinary processes with *compound* expressions, including simple cases of resolution into factors, and the treatment of fractions, naturally follow the third chapter. The immediate succession of topics that require similar work is of the highest importance to the beginner, and it is hoped that the half-dozen chapters on algebraic expressions will prove interesting, and give sufficient readiness in the use of symbols.

A chapter on fractional equations with one unknown number, a chapter on simultaneous equations with two unknown numbers, and a chapter on quadratics follow in order. Only one method of elimination is given in simultaneous equations and one method of completing the square in quadratics. Moreover, the solution of the examples in quadratics requires the square roots of only small numbers such as every pupil knows who has learned the multiplication table. In each of these three chapters a considerable number of problems is given to *state* and solve. By this means the learner is led to exercise his reasoning faculty, and to realize that the methods of Algebra require a strictly logical process. These problems, however, are divided into classes, and a model solution of an example of each class is given as a guide to the solution of other examples of that class.

The course may end with the chapter on quadratics, but the

simple questions of arithmetical progression and of geometrical progression are so interesting in themselves, and show so clearly the power of Algebra, that it will be a great loss not to take the short chapters on these series.

The last chapter is on square and cube roots. It is expected that pupils who use this book will learn how to extract the square and cube roots by the simple formulas of Algebra, and be spared the necessity of committing to memory the long and tedious rules given in Arithmetic, rules that are generally forgotten in less time than they are learned.

Any corrections or suggestions will be thankfully received by the author.

A teachers' edition is in press, containing solutions of examples, and such suggestions as experience with beginners has shown to be valuable.

G. A. WENTWORTH.

EXETER, NH, April, 1894

CONTENTS.

FIRST STEPS IN ALGEBRA.

CHAPTER I.

INTRODUCTION.

NOTE. The principal definitions are put at the beginning of the book for convenient reference. They are not to be committed to memory. It is a good plan to have definitions and explanations read aloud in the class, and to encourage pupils to make comments upon them, and ask questions about them.

1. Algebra. Algebra, like Arithmetic, treats of numbers.

2. Units. In counting separate objects or in measuring magnitudes, the *standards* by which we count or measure are called **units**.

Thus, in counting the boys in a school, the unit is a boy; in selling eggs by the dozen, the unit is a dozen eggs; in selling bricks by the thousand, the unit is a thousand bricks; in measuring short distances, the unit is an inch, a foot, or a yard; in measuring long distances, the unit is a rod or a mile.

3. Numbers. *Repetitions of the unit* are expressed by numbers.

4. Quantities. A number of specified units of any kind is called a quantity; as, 4 pounds, 5 oranges.

5. Number-Symbols in Arithmetic. Arithmetic employs the arbitrary symbols, 1, 2, 3, 4, 5, 6, 7, 8, 9, 0, called **figures**, to represent numbers.

6. Number-Symbols in Algebra. Algebra employs *the letters of the alphabet* in addition to the figures of Arithmetic to represent numbers. Letters are used as *general* symbols of numbers to which *any particular values* may be assigned.

PRINCIPAL SIGNS OF OPERATIONS.

7. The signs of the fundamental operations are the same in Algebra as in Arithmetic.

8. The Sign of Addition, +. The sign + is read *plus*.

Thus, $4 + 3$, read 4 plus 3, indicates that the number 3 is to be added to the number 4, $a + b$, read a plus b, indicates that the number b is to be added to the number a.

9. The Sign of Subtraction, −. The sign − is read *minus*.

Thus, $4 - 3$, read 4 minus 3, indicates that the number 3 is to be subtracted from the number 4, $a - b$, read a minus b, indicates that the number b is to be subtracted from the number a.

10. The Sign of Multiplication, ×. The sign × is read *times*.

Thus, 4×3, read 4 times 3, indicates that the number 3 is to be multiplied by 4, $a \times b$, read a times b, indicates that the number b is to be multiplied by the number a.

A dot is sometimes used for the sign of multiplication. Thus $2 \cdot 3 \cdot 4 \cdot 5$ means the same as $2 \times 3 \times 4 \times 5$. Either sign is read *multiplied by* when followed by the multiplier. $\$a \times b$, or $\$a \cdot b$, is read a dollars multiplied by b.

11. The Sign of Division, $\div$. The sign $\div$ is read *divided by*.

Thus, $4 \div 2$, read 4 divided by 2, indicates that the number 4 is to be divided by 2, $a \div b$, read a divided by b, indicates that the number a is to be divided by the number b.

Division is also indicated by writing the dividend above the divisor with a horizontal line between them.

Thus, $\frac{4}{2}$ means the same as $4 \div 2$; $\frac{a}{b}$ means the same as $a \div b$.

OTHER SIGNS USED IN ALGEBRA.

12. The Sign of Equality, $=$. The sign $=$ is read *is equal to*, when placed between two numbers and indicates that these two numbers are equal.

Thus, $8+4=12$ means that $8+4$ and 12 stand for *equal* numbers; $x+y=20$ means that $x+y$ and 20 stand for equal numbers.

13. The Sign of Inequality, $>$ or $<$. The sign $>$ or $<$ is read *is greater than* and *is less than* respectively, and when placed between two numbers indicates that these two numbers are unequal, and that the number toward which the sign opens is the greater.

Thus, $9+6 > 12$ means that $9+6$ is greater than 12; and $9+6 < 16$ means that $9 + 6$ is less than 16.

14. The Sign of Deduction, $\therefore$ The sign $\therefore$ is read *hence* or *therefore*.

15. The Sign of Continuation, ... The sign ... is read *and so on*.

16. The Signs of Aggregation. The signs of aggregation are the bar |, the vinculum $\overline{}$, the parenthesis ( ), the bracket [ ], and the brace { }.

Thus, each of the expressions $\begin{array}{r} a \\ +b \end{array}\Big|$, $\overline{a+b}$, $(a+b)$, $[a+b]$, $\{a+b\}$, signifies that $a + b$ is to be treated as a single number.

FACTORS. COEFFICIENTS. POWERS.

17. Factors. When a number consists of the product of two or more numbers, each of these numbers is called a **factor** of the product.

The sign $\times$ is generally omitted between a figure and a letter, or between letters; thus, instead of $63 \times a \times b$, we write $63ab$; instead of $a \times b \times c$, we write abc.

The expression abc must not be confounded with $a + b + c$. abc is a product; $a + b + c$ is a sum.

If $\qquad a = 2, \quad b = 3, \quad c = 4,$

then $\qquad abc = 2 \times 3 \times 4 = 24;$

but $\qquad a + b + c = 2 + 3 + 4 = 9.$

NOTE. When a sign of operation is omitted in the notation of Arithmetic, it is always the *sign of addition*; but when a sign of operation is omitted in the notation of Algebra, it is always the *sign of multiplication*. Thus, 456 means $400 + 50 + 6$, but $4ab$ means $4 \times a \times b$.

18. Factors expressed by letters are called **literal** factors; factors expressed by figures are called **numerical** factors.

19. If one factor of a product is equal to 0, the product is equal to 0, whatever the values of the other factors. Such a factor is called a **zero factor**.

20. Coefficients. A known factor of a product which is prefixed to another factor, to show the number of times that factor is taken, is called a **coefficient**.

Thus, in $7c$, 7 is the coefficient of c; in $7ax$, 7 is the coefficient of ax, or, if a is known, $7a$ is the coefficient of x.

By coefficient, we generally mean the **numerical coefficient with its sign**. If no numerical coefficient is written, 1 is understood. Thus, ax means the same as $1ax$.

21. Powers and Roots. A product consisting of two or more **equal factors** is called a **power** of that factor, and one of the equal factors is called a **root** of the number.

Thus, $9 = 3 \times 3$; that is, 9 is a power of 3, and 3 is a root of 9.

22. Indices or Exponents. An index or exponent is a number-symbol written at the right of, and a little above, a number.

If the index is a *whole number*, it shows the number of times the given number is taken as a factor.

Thus, a^1, or simply a, denotes that a is taken *once* as a factor; a^2 denotes that a is taken *twice* as a factor; a^3 denotes that a is taken *three times* as a factor; and a^4 denotes that a is taken *four times* as a factor; and so on. These are read: the first power of a; the second power of a; the third power of a; the fourth power of a; and so on.

a^3 is written instead of aaa.

a^4 is written instead of $aaaa$.

23. The meaning of coefficient and exponent must be carefully distinguished. Thus,

$$4a = a + a + a + a;$$
$$a^4 = a \times a \times a \times a.$$

If $a = 3$,
$$4a = 3 + 3 + 3 + 3 = 12.$$
$$a^4 = 3 \times 3 \times 3 \times 3 = 81.$$

The second power of a number is generally called the *square* of that number; thus, a^2 is called the *square* of a, because if a denotes the number of units of length in the side of a square, a^2 denotes the number of units of surface in the square. The third power of a number is generally called the *cube* of that number; thus, a^3 is called the *cube* of a, because if a denotes the number of units of length in the edge of a cube, a^3 denotes the number of units of volume in the cube.

ALGEBRAIC EXPRESSIONS.

24. An Algebraic Expression. An algebraic expression is a number written with algebraic symbols. An algebraic expression may consist of one symbol, or of several symbols connected by signs.

Thus, a, $3abc$, $5a + 2b - 3c$, are algebraic expressions.

25. Terms. A **term** is an algebraic expression, the parts of which are not separated by the sign + or −.

Thus, a, $5xy$, $2ab \times 4cd$, $\frac{3ab}{4cd}$ are algebraic expressions of one term each. A term may be separated into parts by the sign × or ÷.

26. Simple Expressions. An algebraic expression of *one term* is called a **simple expression** or **monomial**.

Thus, $5xy$, $7a \times 2b$, $7a \div 2b$, are simple expressions.

27. Compound Expressions. An algebraic expression of *two or more terms* is called a **compound expression** or **polynomial**.

Thus, $5xy + 7a$, $2x - y - 3z$, $4a - 3b + 2c - 3d$ are compound expressions.

28. A polynomial of two terms is called a **binomial**; of three terms, a **trinomial**.

Thus, $3a - b$ is a binomial; and $3a - b + c$ is a trinomial.

29. Positive and Negative Terms. The terms of a compound expression preceded by the sign + are called **positive**

terms, and the terms preceded by the sign − are called **negative terms**. The sign + before the first term is omitted.

30. A positive and a negative term of the same numerical value cancel each other when combined.

31. Like Terms. Terms which have the same combination of *letters* are called **like** or **similar** terms; terms which do not have the same combination of letters are called **unlike** or **dissimilar** terms.

Thus, $5a^2bc$, $-7a^2bc$, a^2bc, are like terms; but $5a^2bc$, $5ab^2c$, $5abc^2$, are unlike terms.

32. Degree of a Term. A term that is the product of three letters is said to be of the *third degree*; a term of four letters is of the *fourth degree*; and so on.

Thus, $5abc$ is of the third degree; $2a^2b^2c^2$, that is, $2aabbcc$, is of the sixth degree.

33. Degree of a Compound Expression. The degree of a compound expression is the degree of that term of the expression which is of the *highest degree.*

Thus, $a^2x^2 + bx + c$ is of the fourth degree, since a^2x^2 is of the fourth degree.

34. Dominant Letter. It often happens that there is one letter in an expression of more importance than the rest, and this is, therefore, called the **dominant letter**. In such cases the degree of the expression is generally called by the degree of the *dominant letter.*

Thus, $a^2x^2 + bx + c$ is of the *second degree in x.*

35. Arrangement of a Compound Expression. A compound expression is said to be *arranged* according to the powers of some letter when the exponents of that letter, reckoning from left to right, either descend or ascend in *the order of magnitude.*

Thus, $3ax^3 - 4bx^2 - 6ax + 8b$ is arranged according to the descending powers of x, and $8b - 6ax - 4bx^2 + 3ax^3$ is arranged according to the ascending powers of x.

PARENTHESES.

36. If a compound expression is to be treated as a whole, it is enclosed in a parenthesis.

Thus, $2 \times (10 + 5)$ means that we are to add 5 to 10 and multiply the result by 2; if we were to omit the parenthesis and write $2 \times 10 + 5$, the meaning would be that we were to multiply 10 by 2 and add 5 to the result.

Like the parenthesis, we use with the same meaning any other sign of aggregation.

Thus, $(5 + 2)$, $[5 + 2]$, $\{5 + 2\}$, $\overline{5 + 2}$, $\left.\begin{array}{r}5\\+2\end{array}\right|$, all mean that the expression $5 + 2$ is to be treated as the single symbol 7.

37. Parentheses preceded by +. If a man has 10 dollars and afterwards collects 3 dollars and then 2 dollars, it makes no difference whether he adds the 3 dollars to his 10 dollars, and then the 2 dollars, or puts the 3 and 2 dollars together and adds their sum to his 10 dollars.

The first process is represented by $10 + 3 + 2$.

The second process is represented by $10 + (3 + 2)$.

Hence, $$10 + (3 + 2) = 10 + 3 + 2. \tag{1}$$

If a man has 10 dollars and afterwards collects 3 dollars and then pays a bill of 2 dollars, it makes no difference whether he adds the 3 dollars collected to his 10 dollars and pays out of this sum his bill of 2 dollars, or pays the 2 dollars from the 3 dollars collected and adds the remainder to his 10 dollars.

The first process is represented by $10 + 3 - 2$.

The second process is represented by $10 + (3 - 2)$.

Hence, $$10 + (3 - 2) = 10 + 3 - 2. \tag{2}$$

From (1) and (2) it follows that

If an expression within a parenthesis is preceded by the sign +, the parenthesis can be removed without making any change in the signs of the expression.

CONVERSELY. *Any part of an expression can lie enclosed within a parenthesis and the sign + prefixed, without making any change in the signs of the terms thus enclosed.*

38. Parentheses preceded by −. If a man has 10 dollars and has to pay two bills, one of 3 dollars and one of 2 dollars, it makes no difference whether he takes 3 dollars and 2 dollars in succession, or takes the 3 and 2 dollars at one time, from his 10 dollars.

The first process is represented by $10 - 3 - 2$.

The second process is represented by $10 - (3 + 2)$.

Hence, $$10 - (3 + 2) = 10 - 3 - 2. \quad (3)$$

If a man has 10 dollars consisting of 2 five-dollar bills, and has a debt of 3 dollars to pay, he can pay his debt by giving a five-dollar bill and receiving 2 dollars.

This process is represented by $10 - 5 + 2$.

Since the debt paid is 3 dollars, that is, $(5 - 2)$ dollars, the number of dollars he has left can evidently be expressed by

$$10 - (5 - 2).$$

Hence, $$10 - (5 - 2) = 10 - 5 + 2. \quad (4)$$

From (3) and (4) it follows that

If an expression within a parenthesis is preceded by the sign $-$, *the parenthesis can be removed, provided the sign before each term within the parenthesis is changed, the sign* $+$ *to* $-$, *and the sign* $-$ *to* $+$.

CONVERSELY. *Any part of an expression can be enclosed within a parenthesis and the sign* $-$ *prefixed, provided the sign of each term enclosed is changed, the sign* $+$ *to* $-$, *and the sign* $-$ *to* $+$.

Exercise 1.

Remove the parentheses, and combine:

1. $9 + (3 + 2)$.

2. $9 + (3 - 2)$.

3. $7 + (5 + 1)$.

4. $7 + (5 - 1)$.

5. $6 + (4 + 3)$.

6. $6 + (4 - 3)$.

7. $3 + (8 - 2)$.

8. $9 - (8 - 6)$.

9. $10 - (9 - 5)$.

10. $9 - (6 + 1)$.

11. $8 - (3 + 2)$.

12. $7 - (3 - 2)$.

13. $9 - (4 + 3)$.

14. $9 - (4 - 3)$.

15. $7 - (5 - 2)$.

16. $7 - (7 - 3)$.

17. $(8 - 6) - 1$.

18. $(3 - 2) - (1 - 1)$.

19. $(7 - 3) - (3 - 2)$.

20. $(8 - 2) - (5 - 3)$.

21. $15 - (10 - 3 - 2)$.

39. Multiplying a Compound Expression. The expression $4(5 + 3)$ means that we are to take the sum of the numbers 5 and 3 four times. The process can be represented by placing five dots in a line, and a little to the right three more dots in the same line, and then placing a second, third, and fourth line of dots underneath the first line and exactly similar to it.

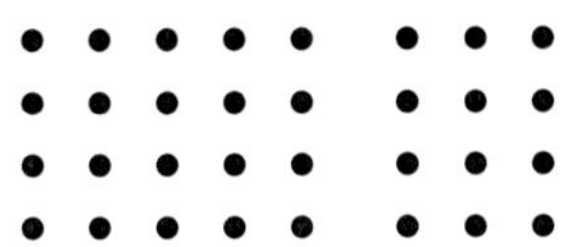

There are $(5 + 3)$ dots in each line, and 4 lines. The total number of dots, therefore, is $4 \times (5 + 3)$.

We see that in the left-hand group there are 4×5 dots, and in the right-hand group 4×3 dots. The sum of these two numbers $(4 \times 5) + (4 \times 3)$ must be equal to the total number; that is,

$$\begin{aligned} 4(5 + 3) &= (4 \times 5) + (4 \times 3) \\ &= 20 + 12. \end{aligned}$$

Again, the expression $4(8 - 3)$ means that we are to take the difference of the numbers 8 and 3 four times. The process can be represented by placing eight dots in a line and crossing the last three, and then placing a second, third, and fourth line of dots underneath the first line and exactly similar to it.

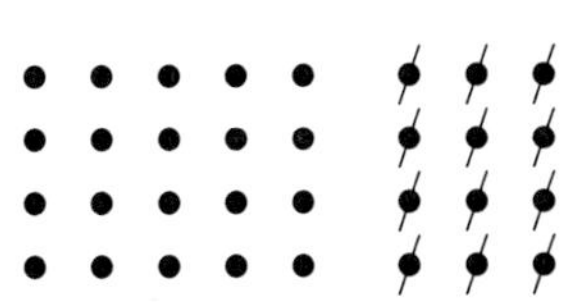

The whole number of dots not crossed in each line is evidently $(8 - 3)$, and the whole number of lines is 4. Therefore the total number of dots not crossed is

$$4 \times (8 - 3).$$

The total number of dots (crossed and not crossed) is (4×8), and the total number of dots crossed is (4×3). Therefore the total number of dots not crossed is

$$(4 \times 8) - (4 \times 3);$$

that is,

$$4(8-3) = (4 \times 8) - (4 \times 3) = 32 - 12.$$

If a, b, and c stand for any three numbers, we have

$$a(b+c) = ab + ac,$$

and

$$a(b-c) = ab - ac.$$ Therefore,

To multiply a compound expression by a simple one,

Multiply each term by the multiplier, and write the successive products with the same signs as those of the original terms.

Exercise 2.

Multiply and remove parentheses:

1. $7(8+5)$. **5.** $8(7+5)$. **9.** $4(a-b)$.

2. $7(8-5)$. **6.** $8(7-5)$. **10.** $2(a^2+b^2)$.

3. $6(7+3)$. **7.** $9(6-2)$. **11.** $2(a^2-b^2)$.

4. $6(7-3)$. **8.** $4(a+b)$. **12.** $3(ab+c)$.

13. $3(ab - c)$.

14. $3(c - ab)$.

15. $a(b + c)$.

16. $a(b - c)$.

17. $3a(b + c)$.

18. $3a(b - c)$.

19. $5a(b^2 + c)$.

20. $5a(b^2 - c^2)$.

21. $5a^2(b^2 - c)$.

40. The numerical value of an algebraic expression is the number obtained by putting for the letters involved the numbers for which these letters stand, and then performing the operations required by the signs.

1. If $b = 4$, find the value of $3b^2$.

Here $$3b^2 = 3 \times 4^2 = 3 \times 16 = 48.$$

2. If $a = 7$, $b = 2$, $c = 3$, find the value of $5ab^2c^3$.

Here $$5ab^2c^3 = 5 \times 7 \times 2^2 \times 3^3 = 3780.$$

Exercise 3.

If $a = 7$, $b = 5$, $c = 3$, find the value of

1. $9a$.

2. $8ab$.

3. $4b^2c$.

4. $2a^2$.

5. $3c^3$.

6. $2b^4$.

7. $5ac$.

8. abc.

9. abc^2.

10. $\frac{1}{3}abc$.

11. $\frac{1}{5}ab^2c$.

12. $\frac{1}{7}a^2bc$.

If $a = 5$, $b = 2$, $c = 0$, $x = 1$, $y = 3$, find the value of

13. $4acy^2$.

14. $3ax^5y^2$.

15. $2ab^2y$.

16. $2a^2b^2c^2y^2$.

17. $2a^2b^2x^2y^2$.

18. $2abx^3y^3$.

19. $3abcxy$.

20. $3abx^3y^2$.

21. $3ab^2xy^2$.

41. The Numerical Value of a Compound Expression.

If a stands for 10, b for 4, and c for 3, find the value of the expression $5ab - 10c^2 - 5b^2$.

Find the value of each term, and combine the results.

$$
\begin{aligned}
5ab \text{ stands for } 5 \times 10 \times 4 &= 200;\\
10c^2 \text{ stands for } \quad 10 \times 3^2 &= \ \ 90;\\
5b^2 \text{ stands for } \quad 5 \times 4^2 &= \ \ 80.
\end{aligned}
$$

$$
\begin{aligned}
\therefore\ & 5ab - 10c^2 - 5b^2\\
&= 200 - 90 - 80\\
&= 30.
\end{aligned}
$$

42. In finding the value of a compound expression the operations indicated *for each term* must be performed *before* the operation indicated by the sign prefixed to the term.

When there is no sign expressed between single symbols or between *simple* and *compound expressions*, it must be remembered that the sign understood is the *sign of multiplication.* Thus $2(a - b)$ has the same meaning as $2 \times (a - b)$.

Exercise 4.

If $a = 5$, $b = 4$, $c = 3$, find the value of

1. $9a - 2bc$.

2. $ab + 2c$.

3. $abc + bc$.

4. $5ac + 2a$.

5. $2abc - 2ac^2$.

6. $ab + bc - ac$.

7. $ac - (b + c)$.

8. $a^2 + (b^2 + c^2)$.

9. $2a + (2b + 2c)$.

10. $a^2 - b^2 - c^2$.

11. $3(a - b + c)$.

12. $6ab - (bc + 8)$.

13. $7bc - c^2 + a$.

14. $5ac - b^2 + 3b$.

15. $4b^2c - 5c^2 - 2b$.

16. $2a + (b + c)$.

17. $b + 2(a - c)$.

18. $c + 2(a - b)$.

19. $2a - (b + c)$.

20. $2b - (a - c)$.

21. $2c - (a - b)$.

22. $2c - 5(a - b)$.

23. $2b - 3(a - c)$.

24. $2c - b(a - b)$.

ALGEBRAIC NOTATION.

Exercise 5.

1. Read $a + b$; $a - b$; ab; $a \div b$.

2. Write six increased by four. $6 + 4$. *Ans.*

3. Write a increased by b.

4. Write six diminished by four. $6 - 4$. *Ans.*

5. Write a diminished by b.

6. By how much does twenty-five exceed sixteen? $25 - 16$. *Ans.*

7. By how much does x exceed y?

8. Write four times three; the fourth power of three. 4×3; 3^4. *Ans.*

9. Write four times x; the fourth power of x.

10. If one part of twenty-five is fifteen, what is the other part? $25 - 15$. *Ans.*

11. If one part of 35 is x, what is the other part?

12. If one part of x is a, what is the other part?

13. How much does ten lack of being twelve? $12 - 10$. *Ans.*

14. How much does x lack of being fourteen?

15. How much does x lack of being a?

16. If a man walks four miles an hour, how many miles will he walk in three hours? 3×4. *Ans.*

17. If a man walks y miles an hour, how many miles will he walk in x hours?

18. If a man walks y miles an hour, how many hours will it take him to walk x miles?

Exercise 6.

1. If the dividend is twenty and the quotient five, what is the divisor? $\frac{20}{5}$. *Ans.*

2. If the dividend is a and the quotient b, what is the divisor?

3. If John is twenty years old to-day, how old was he four years ago? How old will he be five years hence?
$20 - 4$; $20 + 5$. *Ans.*

4. If James is x years old to-day, how old was he three years ago? How old will he be seven years hence?

5. Write four times the expression seven minus five.
$4(7 - 5)$. *Ans.*

6. Write seven times the expression $2x$ minus y.

7. Write the next integral number above four. $4 + 1$. *Ans.*

8. If x is an integral number, write the next integral number above it; the next integral number below it.

9. What number is less than 20 by d?

10. If the difference of two numbers is five, and the smaller number is fifteen, what is the greater number? $15 + 5$. *Ans.*

11. If the difference of two numbers is eight, and the smaller number is x, what is the greater number?

12. If the sum of two numbers is 30, and one of them is 20, what is the other? $30 - 20$. *Ans.*

13. If the sum of two numbers is x, and one of them is 10, what is the other?

14. If 100 contains x ten times, what is the value of x?

Exercise 7.

1. In x years a man will be 40 years old; what is his present age?

2. How old will a man be in y years, if his present age is a years?

3. What is the value of x if $7x$ equals 28?

4. If it takes 3 men 4 days to reap a field, how many days will it take one man to reap it? 3×4. *Ans.*

5. If it takes a men b days to reap a field, how many days will it take one man to reap it?

6. What is the excess of $5x$ over $3x$?

7. By how much does $20 - 3$ exceed $(10 + 1)$?
$20 - 3 - (10 + 1)$. *Ans.*

8. By how much does $2x - 3$ exceed $(x + 1)$?

9. If x stands for 10, find the value of $4(3x - 20)$.

10. If a stands for 10, and b for 2, find the value of $2(a - 2b)$.

11. How many cents in a dollars, b quarters, and c dimes?

12. A book-shelf contains French, Latin, and Greek books. There are 100 books in all, and there are x Latin and y Greek books. How many French books are there?

13. A regiment of men is drawn up in 10 ranks of 80 men each, and there are 15 men over. How many men are there in the regiment? $10 \times 80 + 15$. *Ans.*

14. A regiment of men is drawn up in x ranks of y men each, and there are c men over. How many men are there in the regiment?

Exercise 8.

1. A room is 10 yards long and 8 yards wide. In the middle there is a carpet 6 yards square. How many square yards of oilcloth will be required to cover the rest of the floor?
$10 \times 8 - 6^2$. *Ans.*

2. A room is x yards long and y yards wide. In the middle there is a carpet a yards square. How many square yards of oilcloth will be required to cover the rest of the floor?

3. How many rolls of paper g feet long and k feet wide will be required to paper a room, the perimeter of which, after proper allowance is made for doors and windows, is p feet and the height h feet?

4. Write six times the square of m, plus five c times the expression d plus b minus a.

5. Write five times the expression two n plus one, diminished by six times the expression c minus a plus b.

6. A lady bought a dress for a dollars, a cloak for b dollars, two pairs of gloves for c dollars a pair. She gave a hundred-dollar bill in payment. How much money should be returned to her?

7. If a man can perform a piece of work in 4 days, how much of it can he do in one day? $\frac{1}{4}$. *Ans.*

8. If a man can perform a piece of work in x days, how much of it can he do in one day?

9. If A can do a piece of work in x days, B in y days, C in z days, how much of it can they all do in one day, working together?

10. Write an expression for the sum, and also for the product, of three consecutive numbers of which the least is n.

11. The product of two factors is 36; if one of the factors is x, what is the other factor?

12. If d is the divisor and q the quotient, what is the dividend?

13. If d is the divisor, q the quotient, and r the remainder, what is the dividend?

14. If x oranges can be bought for 50 cents, how many oranges can be bought for 100 cents?

15. What is the price in cents of x apples, if they are ten cents a dozen?

16. If b oranges cost 6 cents, what will a oranges cost?

17. How many miles between two places, if a train travelling m miles an hour requires 4 hours to make the journey?

18. If a man was x years old 10 years ago, how many years old will he be 7 years hence?

19. If a man was x years old y years ago, how many years old will he be c years hence?

20. If a floor is $3x$ yards long and 12 yards wide, how many square yards does the floor contain?

21. How many hours will it take to walk c miles, at the rate of one mile in 15 minutes?

22. Write three consecutive numbers of which x is the middle number.

23. If an odd number is represented by $2n + 1$, what will represent the next odd number?

CHAPTER II.

SIMPLE EQUATIONS.

43. Equations. An equation is a statement in symbols that two expressions stand for the same number.

Thus, the equation $3x + 2 = 8$ states that $3x + 2$ and 8 stand for the same number.

44. That part of the equation which precedes the sign of equality is called the **first member**, or **left side**, and that which follows the sign of equality is called the **second member**, or **right side**.

45. The statement of equality between two algebraic expressions, if true for all values of the letters involved, is called an **identical equation**; but if true only for certain particular values of the letters involved, it is called an **equation of condition**.

Thus, $a + b = b + a$, which is true for *all values* of a and b, is an *identical equation*, and $3x + 2 = 8$, which is true only when x stands for 2, is an *equation of condition*.

For brevity, an identical equation is called an **identity**, and an equation of condition is called simply an **equation**.

46. We often employ an equation to discover an *unknown number* from its relation to known numbers. We usually represent the unknown number by one of the *last* letters of the alphabet, as x, y, z; and by way of distinction, we use the *first* letters, a, b, c, etc., to represent numbers that are supposed to be known, though not expressed in the number-symbols of Arithmetic.

Thus, in the equation $ax + b = c$, x is supposed to represent an unknown number, and a, b, and c are supposed to represent known numbers.

47. Simple Equations. An equation which contains the first power of x, the symbol for the unknown number, and no higher power, is called a **simple equation**, or an **equation of the first degree**.

Thus, $ax + b = c$ is a simple equation, or an equation of the first degree *in* x.

48. Solution of an Equation. To solve an equation is to find the unknown number; that is, the number which, when substituted for its symbol in the given equation, renders the equation an identity. This number is said to *satisfy* the equation, and is called the **root** of the equation.

49. Axioms. In solving an equation, we make use of the following axioms:

Ax. 1. If equal numbers be added to equal numbers, the sums will be equal.

Ax. 2. If equal numbers be subtracted from equal numbers, the remainders will be equal.

Ax. 3. If equal numbers be multiplied by equal numbers, the products will be equal.

Ax. 4. If equal numbers be divided by equal numbers, the quotients will be equal.

If, therefore, the two sides of an equation be increased by, diminished by, multiplied by, or divided by equal numbers, the results will be equal.

Thus, if $8x = 24$, then $8x + 4 = 24 + 4$, $8x - 4 = 24 - 4$, $4 \times 8x = 4 \times 24$, and $8x \div 4 = 24 \div 4$.

50. Transposition of Terms. It becomes necessary in solving an equation to bring all the terms that contain the symbol for the unknown number to one side of the equation, and all the other terms to the other side. This is called **transposing the terms**. We will illustrate by examples:

1. Find the number for which x stands when

$$14x - 11 = 5x + 70.$$

The first object to be attained is to get all the terms which contain x on the left side of the equation, and all the other terms on the right side. This can be done by first subtracting $5x$ from both sides (Ax. 2), which gives

$$9x - 11 = 70,$$

and then adding 11 to these equals (Ax. 1), which gives

$$9x + 11 - 11 = 70 + 11.$$

Combine, $9x = 81.$

Divide by 9, $x = 9.$

2. Find the number for which x stands when $x + b = a$.

The equation is $x + b = a$.

Subtract b from each side, $x + b - b = a - b$. (Ax. 2)

Since $+b$ and $-b$ in the left side cancel each other (§ 30), we have $x = a - b$.

3. Find the number for which x stands when $x - b = a$.

The equation is $x - b = a$.

Add $+b$ to each side, $x + b - b = a + b$. (Ax. 1)

Since $+b$ and $-b$ in the left side cancel each other (§ 30), we have $x = a + b$.

51. The effect of the operation in the preceding equations, when Axioms (1) and (2) are used, is to take a term from one side and put it on the other side with its sign changed. We can proceed in a like manner in any other case. Hence the general rule:

52. *Any term may be transposed from one side of an equation to the other, provided its sign is changed.*

53. Any term, therefore, which occurs on both sides with *the same sign* may be removed from both without affecting the equality; and the sign of every term of an equation may be changed without affecting the equality.

54. Verification. When the root is substituted for its symbol in the given equation, and the equation reduces to an *identity*, the root is said to be **verified**. We will illustrate by examples:

1. What number added to twice itself gives 24?

Let x stand for the number;
then $2x$ will stand for twice the number,
and the number added to twice itself will be $x + 2x$.

But the number added to twice itself is 24.

$$\therefore x + 2x = 24.$$

Combine x and $2x$, $$3x = 24.$$

Divide by 3, the coefficient of x,

$$x = 8. \qquad \text{(Ax. 4)}$$

Therefore the required number is 8.

VERIFICATION.
$$x + 2x = 24,$$
$$8 + 2 \times 8 = 24,$$
$$8 + 16 = 24,$$
$$24 = 24.$$

2. If $4x - 5$ stands for 19, for what number does x stand?

We have the equation

$$4x - 5 = 19.$$

Transpose -5, $\quad 4x = 19 + 5.$

Combine, $\quad 4x = 24.$

Divide by 4, $\quad x = 6. \quad$ (Ax. 4)

VERIFICATION. $\quad 4x - 5 = 19,$

$$4 \times 6 - 5 = 19,$$

$$24 - 5 = 19,$$

$$19 = 19.$$

3. If $3x - 7$ stands for the same number as $14 - 4x$, what number does x stand for?

We have the equation

$$3x - 7 = 14 - 4x.$$

Transpose $-4x$ to the left side, and -7 to the right side,

$$3x + 4x = 14 + 7.$$

Combine, $\quad 7x = 21.$

Divide by 7, $\quad x = 3.$

VERIFICATION. $\quad 3x - 7 = 14 - 4x,$

$$3 \times 3 - 7 = 14 - 4 \times 3,$$

$$2 = 2.$$

4. Solve the equation

$$7(x-1)-30=4(x-4).$$

We have the equation

$$7(x-1)-30=4(x-4).$$

Remove the parentheses,

$$7x-7-30=4x-16.$$

Then $$7x-4x=7+30-16.$$

Combine, $$3x=21.$$

Divide by 3, $$x=7.$$

VERIFICATION. $$7(7-1)-30=4(7-4),$$

$$7\times 6-30=4x3,$$

$$42-30=12,$$

$$12=12.$$

Exercise 9.

Find the number that x stands for, if:

1. $3x=x+8.$

2. $3x=2x+5.$

3. $3x+4=x+10.$

4. $4x+6=x+9.$

5. $7x-19=5x+7.$

6. $3(x-2)=2(x-3).$

7. $8x+7=4x+27.$

8. $3x+10=x+20.$

9. $5(x-2)=3x+4.$

10. $3(x-2)=2(x-1).$

11. $2x+3=16-(2x-3).$

12. $19x-3=2(7+x).$

13. $7x-70=5x-20.$

14. $2x-22=108-2x.$

15. $2(x+5)+5(x-4)=32.$

16. $2(3x-25)=10.$

17. $33x-70=3x+20.$

18. $4(1+x)+3(2+x)=17.$

19. $8x-(x+2)=47.$

20. $3(x-2)=50-(2x-9).$

21. $2x-(3+4x-3x+5)=4.$

22. $5(2-x)+7x-21=x+3.$

23. $3(x-2)+2(x-3)+(x-4)=3x+5.$

24. $x+1+x+2+x+4=2x+12.$

25. $(2x-5)-(x-4)+(x-3)=x-4.$

26. $4-5x-(1-8x)=63-x.$

27. $3x-(x+10)-(x-3)=14-x.$

28. $x^2-2x-3=x^2-3x+1.$

29. $(x^2-9)-(x^2-16)+x=10.$

30. $x^2+8x-(x^2-x-2)=5(x+3)+3.$

31. $x^2+x-2+x^2+2x-3=2x^2-7x-1.$

32. $10x-(x-5)=2x+47.$

33. $7x - 5 - (6 - 8x) + 2 = 3x - 7 + 106.$

34. $6x + 3 - (3x + 2) = (2x - 1) + 9.$

35. $3(x + 10) + 4(x + 20) + 5x - 170 = 15 - 3x.$

36. $20 - x + 4(x - 1) - (x - 2) = 30.$

37. $5x + 3 - (2x - 2) + (1 - x) = 6(9 - x).$

55. Statement and Solution of Problems. The difficulties which the beginner usually meets in stating problems will be quickly overcome if he will observe the following directions:

Study the problem until you clearly understand its meaning and just what is required to be found.

Remember that x must not be put for money, length, time, weight, etc., but for the **required number** of *specified units* of money, length, time, weight, etc.

Express each statement carefully in algebraic language, and write out in full just what each expression stands for.

Do not attempt to form the equation until all the statements are made in symbols.

We will illustrate by examples:

1. John has three times as many oranges as James, and they together have 32. How many has each?

Let x stand for the *number* of oranges James has;

then $3x$ is the number of oranges John has;

and $x + 3x$ is the number of oranges they together have.

But 32 is the number of oranges they together have.

$$\therefore x + 3x = 32;$$

or, $$4x = 32,$$

and $$x = 8.$$

Since $x = 8$, $$3x = 24.$$

Therefore James has 8 oranges, and John has 24 oranges.

NOTE. Beginners in stating the preceding problem generally write:

Let $x =$ *what* James had.

Now, we know *what* James had. He had oranges, and we are to discover simply the *number* of oranges he had.

2. James and John together have \$24, and James has \$8 more than John. How many dollars has each?

Let x stand for the number of dollars John has;
then $x + 8$ is the number of dollars James has;
and $x + (x + 8)$ is the number of dollars they both have.

But 24 is the number of dollars they both have.

$$\therefore x + (x + 8) = 24.$$

Removing the parenthesis,

$$x + x + 8 = 24.$$

$$\therefore 2x = 16.$$

Dividing by 2, $x = 8.$

Since $x = 8$, $x + 8 = 16.$

Therefore John has \$8, and James has \$16.

NOTE. The beginner must avoid the mistake of writing

Let $x =$ John's money.

We are required to find the *number* of dollars John has, and therefore x must represent this required number.

3. The sum of two numbers is 18, and three times the greater number exceeds four times the less by 5. Find the numbers.

Let $x =$ the greater number.

Then, since 18 is the sum and x is one of the numbers, the other number must be the sum minus x. Hence

$18 - x =$ the smaller number.

Now, three times the greater number is $3x$, and four times the less number is $4(18 - x)$.

Hence, $3x - 4(18 - x) =$ the excess.

But $5 =$ the excess,

$$\therefore 3x - 4(18 - x) = 5$$

$$\therefore 3x - (72 - 4x) = 5,$$

or $3x - 72 + 4x = 5.$

$$\therefore 7x = 77,$$

and $x = 11.$

Therefore the numbers are 11 and 7.

Exercise 10.

1. If a number is multiplied by 9, the product is 270. Find the number.

2. If the sum of the ages of a father and son is 60 years, and the father is 5 times as old as the son, what is the age of each?

3. The sum of two numbers is 91, and the greater is 6 times the less. Find the numbers.

4. A tree 90 feet high was broken so that the part broken off was 8 times the length of the part left standing. Find the length of each part.

5. The difference of two numbers is 7, and their sum is 53. Find the numbers.

6. The difference of two numbers is 12, and their sum is 84. Find the numbers.

7. Divide 35 into two parts so that one part shall be greater by 5 than the other part.

8. Three times a given number is equal to the number increased by 40. Find the number.

9. Three times a given number diminished by 24 is equal to the given number. Find the number.

10. One number is 4 times another, and their difference is 30. Find the numbers.

11. The sum of two numbers is 36, and one of them exceeds twice the other by 6. Find the numbers.

HINT. Let x equal the greater number: then $36 - x$ will equal the smaller.

12. The sum of two numbers is 40, and 5 times the smaller exceeds 2 times the greater by 25. Find the numbers.

13. The number 30 is divided into two parts such that 4 times the greater part exceeds 5 times the smaller part by 30. Find the parts.

14. The sum of two numbers is 27, and twice the greater number increased by 3 times the less is 61. Find the numbers.

15. The sum of two numbers is 32, and five times the smaller is 3 times the greater number. Find the numbers.

Exercise 11.

1. A farmer sold a horse and a cow for \$210. He sold the horse for four times as much as the cow. How much did he get for each?

2. Three times the excess of a certain number over 6 is equal to the number plus 144. Find the number.

3. Thirty-one times a certain number is as much above 40 as nine times the number is below 40. Find the number.

4. Two numbers differ by 10, and their sum is equal to seven times their difference. Find the numbers.

5. Find three consecutive numbers, x, $x+1$, and $x+2$, whose sum is 78.

6. Find five consecutive numbers whose sum is 35.

7. The sum of the ages of A and B is 40 years, and 10 years hence A will be twice as old as B. Find their present ages.

8. A father is four times as old as his son, and in 5 years he will be only three times as old. Find their present ages.

9. One man is 60 years old, and another man is 50 years. How many years ago was the first man twice as old as the second?

10. A man 50 years old has a son 10 years old. In how many years will the father be three times as old as the son?

11. A has \$100, and B has \$20. How much must A give B in order that they may each have the same sum?

12. A banker paid \$63 in 5-dollar bills and 2-dollar bills. He paid just as many 5-dollar bills as 2-dollar bills. How many bills of each kind did he pay?

Exercise 12.

1. In a company of 90 persons, composed of men, women, and children, there are three times as many children as men, and twice as many women as men. How many are there of each?

2. Find the number whose double exceeds 70 by as much as the number itself is less than 80.

3. A farmer employed two men to build 112 rods of wall. One of them built on the average 4 rods a day, and the other 3 rods a day. How many days did they work?

4. Two men travel in *opposite* directions, one 30 miles a day, and the other 20 miles a day. In how many days will they be 350 miles apart?

5. Two men travel in the same direction, one 30 miles a day, and the other 20 miles a day. In how many days will they be 350 miles apart?

6. A man bought 3 equal lots of hay for $408. For the first lot he gave $17 a ton, for the second $16, for the third $18. How many tons did he buy in all?

7. A farmer sold a quantity of wood for $84, one half of it at $3 a cord, and the other half at $4 a cord. How many cords did he sell?

HINT. Let $2x$ equal the number of cords.

8. If $2x - 3$ stands for 29, for what number will $4 + x$ stand?

9. At an election two opposing candidates received together 2044 votes, and one received 104 more votes than the other. How many votes did each candidate receive?

Exercise 13.

1. A man walks 4 miles an hour for x hours, and another man walks 3 miles an hour for $x + 2$ hours. If they each walk the same distance, how many miles does each walk?

2. A has twice as much money as B; but if A gives B $30, it will take twice as much as A has left to equal B's. How much money has each?

3. I have $12.75 in two-dollar bills and twenty-five cent pieces, and I have twice as many bills as twenty-five cent pieces. How many have I of each?

4. I have in mind a certain number. If this number is diminished by 8 and the remainder multiplied by 8, the result is the same as if the number was diminished by 6 and the remainder multiplied by 6. What is the number?

5. I have five times as many half-dollars as quarters, and the half-dollars and quarters amount to $11. How many of each have I?

6. A man pays a debt of $91 with ten-dollar bills and one-dollar bills, paying three times as many one-dollar bills as ten-dollar bills. How many bills of each kind does he pay?

7. A father is four times as old as his son, but 4 years hence he will be only three times as old as his son. How old is each?

8. A workman was employed for 24 days. For every day he worked he was to receive \$1.50, and for every day he was idle he was to pay \$0.50 for his board. At the end of the time he received \$28. How many days did he work?

Exercise 14.

1. A boy has 4 hours at his disposal. How far can he ride into the country at the rate of 9 miles an hour and walk back at the rate of 3 miles an hour, if he returns just on time?

HINT. Let $x =$ the number of hours he rides.

Then $4 - x =$ the number he walks.

2. A has \$180, and B has \$80. How much must A give B in order that six times B's money shall be equal to 7 times A's?

3. A grocer has two kinds of tea, one kind worth 45 cents a pound, and the other worth 65 cents a pound. How many pounds of each kind must he take to make 80 pounds, worth 50 cents a pound?

4. A tank holding 1200 gallons has three pipes. The first lets in 8 gallons a minute, the second 10 gallons, and the third 12 gallons a minute. In how many minutes will the tank be filled?

5. The fore and hind wheels of a carriage are 10 feet and 12 feet respectively in circumference. How many feet will the carriage have passed over when the fore wheel has made 250 revolutions more than the hind wheel?

6. Divide a yard of tape into two parts so that one part shall be 6 inches longer than the other part.

7. A boy bought 7 dozen oranges for \$1.50. For a part he paid 20 cents a dozen; and for the remainder, 25 cents a dozen. How many dozen of each kind did he buy?

8. How can a bill of \$3.30 be paid in quarters and ten-cent pieces so as to pay three times as many ten-cent pieces as quarters?

CHAPTER III.

POSITIVE AND NEGATIVE NUMBERS.

56. Quantities Opposite in Kind. If a person is engaged in trade, his capital will be *increased* by his *gains*, and *diminished* by his *losses.*

Increase in temperature is measured by the number of degrees the mercury rises in a thermometer, and *decrease* in temperature by the number of degrees the mercury *falls.*

In considering any quantity whatever, a quantity that *increases* the quantity considered is called a *positive quantity*; and a quantity that *decreases* the quantity considered is called a *negative quantity.*

57. Positive and Negative Numbers. If from a given point, marked 0, we draw a straight line to the right, and beginning from the *zero* point lay off units of length on this line, the successive repetitions of the unit will be expressed by the *natural series of numbers*, 1, 2, 3, 4, etc. Thus:

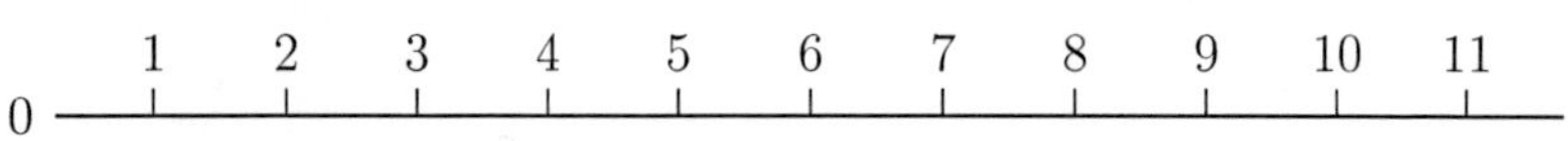

If we wish to *add* 2 to 5, we begin at 5, count 2 units *forwards*, and arrive at 7, the sum required. If we wish to *subtract* 2 from 5, we begin at 5, count 2 units *backwards*, and arrive at 3, the difference required. If we wish to subtract 5 from 5, we count 5 units backwards, and arrive at 0. If we wish to subtract

5 from 2, we cannot do it, because when we have counted backwards from 2 as far as 0, *the natural series of numbers comes to an end.*

In order to subtract a greater number from a smaller, it is necessary to *assume* a new series of numbers, beginning at zero and extending to the left of zero. The series to the left of zero must proceed from zero by *the repetitions of the unit*, precisely like the natural series to the right of zero; and the *opposition* between the right-hand series and the left-hand series must be clearly marked. This opposition is indicated by calling every number in the right-hand series a **positive number**, and prefixing to it, when written, the sign $+$; and by calling every number in the left-hand series a **negative number**, and prefixing to it the sign $-$. The two series of numbers may be called the **algebraic series of numbers**, and written thus:

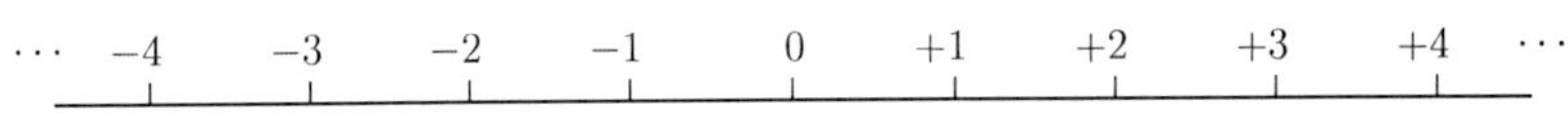

If, now, we wish to subtract 7 from 4, we begin at 4 in the positive series, count 7 units in the *negative direction* (to the left), and arrive at -3 in the negative series; that is, $4-7=-3$.

The result obtained by subtracting a greater number from a less, when both are positive, is *always a negative number.*

In general, if a and b represent any two numbers of the positive series, the expression $a-b$ will be a positive number when a is greater than b; will be zero when a is equal to b; will be a negative number when a is less than b.

In counting from left to right in the algebraic series, numbers *increase* in magnitude; in counting from right to left, numbers *decrease* in magnitude. Thus -3, -1, 0, $+2$, $+4$, are arranged in *ascending* order of magnitude.

58. Every algebraic number, as $+4$ or -4, consists of a *sign* $+$ or $-$ and the *absolute value* of the number. The sign shows whether the number belongs to the positive or negative series of numbers; the absolute value shows the place the number has in the positive or negative series.

When no sign stands before a number, the sign $+$ is always understood. Thus 4 means the same as $+4$, a means the same as $+a$. But *the sign $-$ is never omitted.*

59. Two algebraic numbers which have, one the sign $+$, and the other the sign $-$, are said to have *unlike signs.*

Two algebraic numbers which have the same absolute values, but unlike signs, always cancel each other when combined. Thus $+4-4=0$; $+a-a=0$.

60. Double Meanings of the Signs + and −. The use of the signs $+$ and $-$ to indicate addition and subtraction must be carefully distinguished from the use of the signs $+$ and $-$ to indicate in which series, the positive or the negative, a given number belongs. In the first sense they are signs of *operations*, and are common to Arithmetic and Algebra; in the second sense they are signs of *opposition*, and are employed in Algebra alone.

NOTE. In Arithmetic, if the things counted are *whole units*, the numbers which count them are called **whole numbers**, **integral**

numbers, or **integers**, where the adjective is transferred from the things counted to the numbers which count them. But if the things counted are only *parts of units*, the numbers which count them are called **fractional numbers**, or simply **fractions**, where again the adjective is transferred from the things counted to the numbers which count them.

Likewise in Algebra, if the units counted are *negative*, the numbers which count them are called **negative numbers**, where the adjective which defines the nature of the units counted is transferred to the numbers that count them.

A whole number means a number of whole units, a fractional number means a number of parts of units, and a negative number means a number of negative units.

61. Addition and Subtraction of Algebraic Numbers. An algebraic number which is to be added or subtracted is often enclosed in a parenthesis, in order that the signs + and −, which are used to distinguish positive and negative numbers, may not be confounded with the + and − signs that denote the operations of addition and subtraction. Thus $+4+(-3)$ expresses the sum, and $+4-(-3)$ expresses the difference, of the numbers $+4$ and -3.

62. Addition. In order to add two algebraic numbers, we begin at the place in the series which the first number occupies, and count, *in the direction indicated by the sign of the second number*, as many units as there are in the absolute value of the second number.

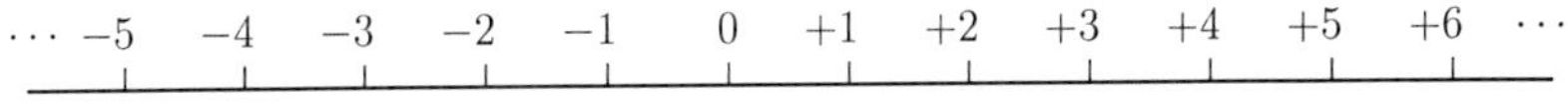

Thus the sum of $+4 + (+3)$ is found by counting from $+4$ three units in *the positive direction*; that is, to the right, and is, therefore, $+7$.

The sum of $+4 + (-3)$ is found by counting from $+4$ three units in *the negative direction*; that is, to the left, and is, therefore, $+1$.

The sum of $-4 + (+3)$ is found by counting from -4 three units in the positive direction, and is, therefore, -1.

The sum of $-4 + (-3)$ is found by counting from -4 three units in the negative direction, and is, therefore, -7.

63. Subtraction. In order to subtract one algebraic number from another, we begin at the place in the series which the minuend occupies, and count, *in the direction opposite to that indicated by the sign of the subtrahend*, as many units as there are in the absolute value of the subtrahend.

Thus the result of subtracting $+3$ from $+4$ is found by counting from $+4$ three units in the *negative direction*; that is, in the direction *opposite to that indicated by the sign + before* 3, and is, therefore, $+1$.

The result of subtracting -3 from $+4$ is found by counting from $+4$ three units in the *positive direction*, and is, therefore, $+7$.

The result of subtracting $+3$ from -4 is found by counting from -4 three units in the *negative direction*, and is, therefore, -7.

The result of subtracting -3 from -4 is found by counting from -4 three units in the *positive direction*, and is, therefore, -1.

64. Collecting the results obtained in addition and subtraction, we have:

ADDITION.	SUBTRACTION.
$+4+(-3)=+4-3=+1.$	$+4-(+3)=+4-3=+1.$
$+4+(+3)=+4+3=+7.$	$+4-(-3)=+4+3=+7.$
$-4+(-3)=-4-3=-7.$	$-4-(+3)=-4-3=-7.$
$-4+(+3)=-4+3=-1.$	$-4-(-3)=-4+3=-1.$

65. From these four cases of addition, therefore,

To Add Algebraic Numbers,

I. *If the numbers have like signs, find the sum of their absolute values, and prefix the common sign to the result.*

II. *If the numbers have unlike signs, find the difference of their absolute values, and prefix the sign of the greater number to the result.*

III. *If there are more than two numbers, find the sum of the positive numbers and the sum of the negative numbers, take the difference between the absolute values of these two sums, and prefix the sign of the greater sum to the result.*

NOTE. Since the order in which numbers are added is immaterial, we may add any two of the numbers, and then this sum to any third number, and so on.

66. The result is generally called the **algebraic sum**, in distinction from the arithmetical sum; that is, the sum of the absolute values of the numbers.

67. From the four cases of subtraction in § 64, we see that *subtracting a positive number is equivalent to adding an equal negative number, and subtracting a negative number is equivalent to adding an equal positive number.*

To Subtract One Algebraic Number from Another,

Change the sign of the subtrahend, and add the subtrahend to the minuend.

68. Examples.

1. Find the sum of $3a$, $2a$, a, $5a$, $7a$.

The sum of the coefficients is $3 + 2 + 1 + 5 + 7 = 18$.

Hence the sum of the numbers is $18a$.

2. Find the sum of $-5c$, $-c$, $-3c$, $-4c$, $-2c$.

The sum of the coefficients is $-5 - 1 - 3 - 4 - 2 = -15$.

Hence the sum of the numbers is $-15c$.

3. Find the sum of $8x$, $-9x$, $-x$, $3x$, $4x$, $-12x$, x.

The sum of the positive coefficients is $8 + 3 + 4 + 1 = 16$.

The sum of the negative coefficients is $-9 - 1 - 12 = -22$.

The difference between 16 and 22 is 6, and the sign of the greater is negative.

Hence the required sum is $-6x$.

Exercise 15.

Find the sum of:

1. $5c$, $23c$, c, $11c$.

2. $4a$, $3a$, $7a$, $10a$.

3. $7x$, $12x$, $11x$, $9x$.

4. $6y$, $8y$, $2y$, $35y$.

5. $-3a$, $-5a$, $-18a$.

6. $-5x$, $-6x$, $-18x$, $-11x$.

7. $-3b$, $-b$, $-9b$, $-4b$.

8. $-z$, $-2z$, $-10z$, $-53z$.

9. $-11m$, $-3m$, $-5m$, $-m$.

10. $5d$, $-d$, $-4d$, $2d$.

11. $13n$, $13n$, $-11n$, $-6n$, $-9n$, n, $2n$, $-3n$.

12. $5g$, $-3g$, $-6g$, $-4g$, $20g$, $-5g$, $-11g$, $-14g$.

13. $-9a^2$, $5a^2$, $6a^2$, a^2, $2a^2$, $-a^2$, $-3a^2$.

14. $3x^3$, $-2x^3$, $-5x^3$, $-7x^3$, $-x^3$, $2x^3$, $-10x^3$, $-x^3$.

15. $4a^2b^2$, $-a^2b^2$, $-6a^2b^2$, $4a^2b^2$, $-2a^2b^2$, a^2b^2.

16. $6mn$, $-5mn$, mn, $-3mn$, $4mn$.

17. $3xyz$, $-2xyz$, $5xyz$, $-7xyz$, xyz.

18. $5a^3b^3c^3$, $-7a^3b^3c^3$, $-3a^3b^3c^3$, $2a^3b^3c^3$.

19. $11abcd$, $-10abcd$, $-9abcd$, $-abcd$.

20. Subtract $-a$ from $-b$, and find the value of the result if $a = -4$, $b = -5$.

When $a = 4$, $b = -2$, $c = -3$, find the difference in the values of:

21. $a - b + c$ and $-a + b + c$.

22. $a + (-b) + c$ and $a - (-b) + c$.

23. $-a - (-b) + c$ and $-(-a) + (-b) - c$.

24. $a - b + (-c)$ and $a - (-b) - (-c)$.

MULTIPLICATION AND DIVISION OF ALGEBRAIC NUMBERS

69. Multiplication. Multiplication is generally defined in Arithmetic as the process of finding the result when one number (the multiplicand) is taken as many times as there are units in another number (the multiplier). This definition fails when the *multiplier is a fraction.* In multiplying by a fraction, we divide the multiplicand into as many equal parts as there are units in the denominator, and take as many of these parts as there are units in the numerator.

If, for example, we multiply 6 by $\frac{2}{3}$, we divide 6 into *three* equal parts and take *two* of these parts, obtaining 4 for the product. The multiplier, $\frac{2}{3}$, is $\frac{2}{3}$ of 1, and the product, 4, is $\frac{2}{3}$ of 6, in other words, *the product is obtained from the multiplicand precisely as the multiplier is obtained from* 1.

This statement is also true when the multiplier is a whole number. Thus in $5 \times 7 = 35$, the multiplier, 5, is equal to

$$1 + 1 + 1 + 1 + 1,$$

and the product, 35, is equal to

$$7 + 7 + 7 + 7 + 7.$$

70. Multiplication may be defined, therefore,

As the operation of finding from two given numbers, called *multiplicand* and *multiplier*, a third number called *product*, which is *formed from the multiplicand as the multiplier is formed from unity*.

71. According to this definition of multiplication,

since
$$+3 = +1 + 1 + 1,$$
$$3 \times (+8) = +8 + 8 + 8 \qquad (1)$$
$$= +24,$$
and
$$3 \times (-8) = -8 - 8 - 8 \qquad (2)$$
$$= -24.$$

Again, since
$$-3 = -1 - 1 - 1;$$
$$(-3) \times 8 = -8 - 8 - 8 \qquad (3)$$
$$= -24,$$
and
$$(-3) \times (-8) = -(-8) - (-8) - (-8) \qquad (4)$$
$$= +8 + 8 + 8$$
$$= +24.$$

72. From these four cases it follows that in finding the product of two algebraic numbers, if the two numbers have *like* signs, the product will have the *plus* sign, and if *unlike* signs, the product will have the *minus* sign.

Hence the **Law of Signs in Multiplication** is:

Like signs give +, and unlike signs give −.

If a and b stand for any two numbers, we have

$$(+a) \times (+b) = +ab,$$
$$(+a) \times (-b) = -ab,$$
$$(-a) \times (+b) = -ab,$$
$$(-a) \times (-b) = +ab.$$

73. The Index Law in Multiplication.

Since $\quad a^2 = aa, \quad$ and $\quad a^3 = aaa,$

$$a^2 \times a^3 = aa \times aaa = aaaaa = a^5 = a^{2+3};$$
$$a^4 \times a = aaaa \times a = aaaaa = a^5 = a^{4+1}.$$

If a stands for any number, and m and n for any integers,

$$a^m \times a^n = a^{m+n}. \quad \text{Hence,}$$

The index of the product of two powers of the same number is equal to the sum of the indices of the factors.

74. Examples.

1. Find the product of $6a^2b^2$ and $7ab^2c^3$.

Since the order of the factors is immaterial,

$$\begin{aligned} 6a^2b^3 \times 7ab^2c^3 &= 6 \times 7 \times a^2 \times a \times b^3 \times b^2 \times c^3 \\ &= 42a^3b^5c^3. \end{aligned}$$

2. Find the product of $-3ab$ and $7ab^3$.

$$\begin{aligned} -3ab \times 7ab^3 &= -3 \times 7 \times a \times a \times b \times b^3 \\ &= -21a^2b^4. \end{aligned}$$

75. To Find the Product of Simple Expressions, therefore,

Take the product of the coefficients and the sum of the indices of the like letters.

Exercise 16.

Find the product of:

1. $5a^2$ and $6a^3$.

2. $8ab$ and $5a^3b^2$.

3. $9xy$ and $7xy$.

4. $2a^2b$ and $a^3b^4c^2$.

5. $3a^3b^7c^8$ and $3a^4b^2c$.

6. $2a$ and $-5a$.

7. $-3a$ and $-4b$.

8. $-ab$ and a^3b^2.

9. $-2ab^4$ and $-5a^4bc$.

10. $-2x^6y^3z$ and $-6xy^2z$.

11. $3a^2b$, $-5ab^2$, and $-7a^4b^2$.

12. $2a^2bc^3$, $-3a^3b^2c$, and $-ab^2c^3$.

13. $2b^2c^2x^2$, $2a^2b^2c^3$, and $-3a^3bx^3$.

14. $2a^3b^2c$, $-3a^2b^3c$, and $-4a^2bc^3$.

15. $7am^2x^3$, $3a^4m^2x^3$, and $-2amx$.

16. $-3x^2y^2z^2$, $2x^2yz^3$, and $-5x^4yz$.

If $a = -2$, $b = 3$, and $c = -1$, find the value of:

17. $2ab^2 - 3bc^2 + c$.

18. $4a^2 - 2b^2 - c^2$.

19. $5a + 2b - 4c^4$.

20. $2a^3 - 3b + 8c^2$.

21. $-a + 3b - 2c^2$.

22. $-a^3 - 2b - 10c$.

23. $3a^3 - 3b^3 - 3c^3$.

24. $2ab^2 - 3bc^2 + 2ac$.

25. $3abc + 5a^2b^2 - 2a^2b$.

26. $ab^2c^2 + 2abc^2 + a^2b^2c^2$.

27. $2a^2bc + 3abc + a^2b^2c^2$.

28. $6a^2 + 8a^2b^2 - 5a^2bc$.

76. Division. To divide 48 by 8 is to find the number of times it is necessary to take 8 to make 48. Here the *product* and *one factor* are given, and *the other factor* is required. We may, therefore, take for the definition of division:

The operation by which when *the product* and *one factor* are given, *the other factor is found.*

With reference to this operation the product is called the **dividend**, the given factor the **divisor**, and the required factor the **quotient**.

77. Law of Signs in Division.

Since $(+a)\times(+b)=+ab$, $\quad\therefore +ab\div(+a)=+b$.

Since $(+a)\times(-b)=-ab$, $\quad\therefore -ab\div(+a)=-b$.

Since $(-a)\times(+b)=-ab$, $\quad\therefore -ab\div(-a)=+b$.

Since $(-a)\times(-b)=+ab$, $\quad\therefore +ab\div(-a)=-b$.

That is, if the dividend and divisor have like signs, the quotient has the plus sign; and if they have unlike signs, the quotient has the minus sign. Hence, in division,

Like signs give +, and unlike signs give −.

78. Index Law in Division.

The dividend contains all the factors of the divisor and of the quotient, and therefore the quotient contains the factors of the dividend that are not found in the divisor.

Thus, $\dfrac{abc}{bc}=a$, $\dfrac{aabx}{ab}=ax$, $\dfrac{124abc}{-4ab}=-31c$.

Divide a^5 by a^2, a^6 by a^4, a^4 by a.

$$\frac{a^5}{a^2}=\frac{aaaaa}{aa}=aaa=a^3=a^{5-2};$$

$$\frac{a^6}{a^4}=\frac{aaaaaa}{aaaa}=aa=a^2=a^{6-4};$$

$$\frac{a^4}{a}=\frac{aaaa}{a}=aaa=a^3=a^{4-1}.$$

If m and n stand for any integers, and m is greater than n,

$$a^m - a^n = a^{m-n}.$$

The index of the quotient of two powers of the same letter is equal to the index of the letter in the dividend diminished by the index of the letter in the divisor.

79. Examples.

1. Divide $15xy$ by $5x$.

$$\frac{15xy}{5x} = \frac{3 \times 5xy}{5x} = 3y.$$

Here we cancel the factors 5 and x, which are common to the dividend and divisor.

2. Divide $-21a^2b^3$ by $3ab^2$.

$$\frac{-21a^2b^3}{3ab^2} = -7ab.$$

3. Divide $54a^5b^3c$ by $-6ab^2c$.

$$\frac{54a^5b^3c}{-6ab^2c} = -9a^4b.$$

4. Divide $-45x^4y^5z^7$ by $-15x^4y^5z^5$.

$$\frac{-45x^4y^5z^7}{-15x^4y^5z^5} = 3z^2.$$

5. Divide $-15a^3b^2c^3$ by $-60a^2bc^3$.

$$\frac{-15a^3b^2c^3}{-60a^2bc^3} = \frac{ab}{4}.$$

Exercise 17.

Divide:

1. x^3 by x.

2. $21x^5$ by $7x^3$.

3. $35x^2$ by $-5x^2$.

4. $-42x^2$ by $6x^2$.

5. $-63x^5$ by $-9x$.

6. $-72x^3$ by $-8x^2$.

7. $-32a^2b^2$ by $8ab^2$.

8. $-16x^3y^3$ by $-4xy$.

9. $18x^2y$ by $-2xy$.

10. $-25x^4y^2$ by $-5x^3y^2$.

11. $-51x^2y^3$ by $-17x^2y$.

12. $-28a^4b^3$ by $7a^3b$.

13. $-36x^2y^6$ by $-3xy^2$.

14. $-3x^4y^6$ by $-5xy^3$.

15. $-12a^2b^3$ by $8ab^3$.

16. $-abcd$ by ac.

17. $-a^2b^3c^4d^5$ by $-ab^3c^3d^3$.

18. $2x^2y^2z^3$ by $-3xyz^3$.

19. $-5a^5b^3c^7$ by $-a^4b^2c^7$.

20. $52a^2m^3n^4$ by $13a^2m^2n^3$.

21. $13xy^2z^4$ by $39xyz$.

22. $68xc^2d^3$ by $-4xcd^2$.

23. $-8m^5n^3p^2$ by $-4m^5np$.

24. $-6pqr^3$ by $-2p^2qr$.

25. $26a^2g^2t^5$ by $-2agt^4$.

26. $-a^4b^2c^3$ by $-a^5b^3c^4$.

27. $-3x^2y^2z^2$ by $-2x^3y^4z^5$.

28. $-6mnp$ by $-3m^2n^2p^2$.

29. $-17a^2b^3c^4$ by $51ab^5c^4$.

30. $-19mg^2t^3$ by $57m2^gt^4$.

CHAPTER IV.

ADDITION AND SUBTRACTION.

Integral Compound Expressions.

80. If an algebraic expression contains only *integral forms*, that is, contains *no letter in the denominator of any of its terms*, it is called an **integral expression**.

Thus, $x^3 + 7cx^2 - c^3 - 5c^2x$, is an integral expression.

Integral and fractional expressions are so named on account of the *form of the expressions*, and with no reference whatever to the *numerical value* of the expressions when definite numbers are put in place of the letters.

81. Addition of Integral Compound Expressions. The addition of two algebraic expressions can be represented by connecting the second expression with the first by the sign $+$. If there are no like terms in the two expressions, the operation is *algebraically complete* when the two expressions are thus connected.

If, for example, it is required to add $m+n-p$ to $a+b+c$, the result will be $a+b+c+(m+n-p)$; or, removing the parenthesis (§ 37), $a+b+c+m+n-p$.

82. If there are like terms in the expressions, the like terms can be *collected*; that is, every set of like terms can be replaced by a single term with a coefficient equal to the algebraic sum of the coefficients of the like terms.

1. Add $6x^2 + 5x + 4$ to $x^2 - 4x - 5$.

$$\begin{aligned}\text{The sum } &= x^2 - 4x - 5 + (6x^2 + 5x + 4)\\ &= x^2 - 4x - 5 + 6x^2 + 5x + 4 \qquad \S\ 37\\ &= x^2 + 6x^2 - 4x + 5x - 5 + 4\\ &= 7x^2 + x - 1.\end{aligned}$$

This process is more conveniently represented by arranging the terms in columns, so that like terms shall stand in the same column, as follows:

$$\begin{array}{r} x^2 - 4x - 5\\ 6x^2 + 5x + 4\\ \hline 7x^2 + x - 1\end{array}$$

The coefficient of x^2 in the result will be $6 + 1$, or 7; the coefficient of x will be $-4 + 5$, or 1; and the last term is $-5 + 4$, or -1.

NOTE. When the coefficient of a term is 1, it is not written, but understood.

2. Add $2c^3 - 5c^2d + 6cd^2 + d^3$; $c^3 + 6c^2d - 5cd^2 - 2d^3$; and $3c^3 - c^2d - 7cd^2 - 3d^3$.

$$\begin{array}{rrrr} 2c^3 & - 5c^2d & + 6cd^2 & + d^3\\ c^3 & + 6c^2d & - 5cd^2 & - 2d^3\\ 3c^3 & - c^2d & - 7cd^2 & - 3d^3\\ \hline 6c^3 & & - 6cd^2 & - 4d^3\end{array}$$

The coefficient of c^3 in the result will be $2 + 1 + 3$, or 6; the coefficient of c^2d will be $-5 + 6 - 1$, or 0; therefore c^2d will not appear in the result; the coefficient of cd^2 will be $6-5-7$, or -6; and the coefficient of d^3 will be $1 - 2 - 3$, or -4.

Exercise 18.

Find the sum of:

1. $a^2 - ab + b^2$; $a^2 + ab + b^2$.

2. $3a^2 + 5a - 7$; $6a^2 - 7a + 13$.

3. $x + 2y - 3z$; $-3x + y + 2z$; $2x - 3y + z$.

4. $3x + 2y - z$; $-x + 3y + 2z$; $2x - y + 3z$.

5. $-3a + 2b + c$; $a - 3b + 2c$; $2a + 3b - c$.

6. $-a + 3b + 4c$; $3a - b + 2c$; $2a + 2b - 2c$.

7. $4a^2 + 3a + 5$; $-2a^2 + 3a - 8$; $a^2 - a + 1$.

8. $5ab + 6bc - 7ac$; $3ab - 9bc + 4ac$; $3bc + 6ac$.

9. $x^3 + x^2 + x$; $2x^3 + 3x^2 - 2x$; $3x^3 - 4x^2 + x$.

10. $3y^2 - x^2 - 3xy$; $5x^2 + 6xy - 7y^2$; $x^2 + 2y^2$.

11. $2a^2 - 2ab + 3b^2$; $4b^2 + 5ab - 2a^2$; $a^2 - 3ab - 9b^2$.

12. $a^3 - a^2 + a - 1$; $a^2 - 2a + 2$; $3a^3 + 7a + 1$.

13. $2m^3 - m^2 - m$; $4m^3 + 8m^2 - 7$; $-3m^3 + m + 9$.

14. $x^3 - 3x + 6y$; $x^2 + 2x - 5y$; $x^3 - 3x^2 + 5x$.

15. $6x^3 - 5x + 1$; $x^3 + 3x + 4$; $7x^2 + 2x - 3$.

16. $a^3 + 3a^2b - 3ab^2$; $-3a^2b - 6ab^2 - b^3$; $3a^2b + 4ab^2$.

17. $a^3 - 2a^2b - 2ab^2$; $a^2b - 3ab^2 - b^3$; $3ab^2 - 2a^3 - b^3$.

18. $7x^3 - 2x^2y + 9xy^2 + 13y^3$; $5x^2y - 4xy^2 - 2x^3 - 3y^3$; $y^3 - x^3 - 3x^2y - 5xy^2$; $2x^2y - 5y^3 - 2x^3 - xy^2$.

19. Show that $x+y+z=0$, if $x=a-b-c$, $y=2b+2c-3a$, and $z=2a-b-c$.

20. Show that $x+y=3z$, if $x=3a^2-6a+12$, $y=9a^2+12a-21$, and $z=4a^2+2a-3$.

83. Subtraction of Integral Compound Expressions. The subtraction of one expression from another, if none of the terms are alike, can be represented only by connecting the subtrahend with the minuend by means of the sign $-$.

If, for example, it is required to subtract $a+b+c$ from $m+n-p$, the result will be represented by

$$m+n-p-(a+b+c);$$

or, removing the parenthesis (§ 38),

$$m+n-p-a-b-c.$$

If, however, some of the terms in the two expressions are alike, we can replace two like terms by a single term.

Thus, suppose it is required to subtract a^3+2a^2+3a-5 from $2a^3-3a^2+2a-1$; the result may be expressed as follows:

$$2a^3-3a^2+2a-1-(a^3+2a^2+3a-5);$$

or, removing the parenthesis (§ 38),

$$\begin{aligned}&2a^3 - 3a^2 + 2a - 1 - a^3 - 2a^2 - 3a + 5\\ &\quad = 2a^3 - a^3 - 3a^2 - 2a^2 + 2a - 3a - 1 + 5\\ &\quad = a^3 - 5a^2 - a + 4.\end{aligned}$$

This process is more easily performed by writing the subtrahend below the minuend, *mentally* changing the sign of each term in the subtrahend, and adding.

$$\begin{array}{r}2a^3 - 3a^2 + 2a - 1\\ a^3 + 2a^2 + 3a - 5\\ \hline a^3 - 5a^2 - a + 4\end{array}$$

By changing the sign of each term in the subtrahend, the coefficient of a^3 will be $2 - 1$, or 1; the coefficient of a^2 will be $-3 - 2$, or -5; the coefficient of a will be $2 - 3$, or -1; the last term will be $-1 + 5$, or 4.

Again, suppose it is required to subtract $x^5 - 2ax^4 - 3a^2x^3 + 4a^3x^2$ from $4a^3x^2 - 2a^2x^3 - 5ax^4$. Here terms which are alike can be written in columns, as before:

$$\begin{array}{rrrr} & -\,5ax^4 & -\,2a^2x^3 & +\,4a^3x^2\\ x^5 & -\,2ax^4 & -\,3a^2x^3 & +\,4a^3x^2\\ \hline -x^5 & -\,3ax^4 & +\,a^2x^3 & \end{array}$$

There is no term of x^5 in the minuend, hence the coefficient of x^5 in the result will be $0 - 1$, or -1; the coefficient of ax^4 will be $-5 + 2$, or -3; the coefficient of a^2x^3 will be $-2 + 3$, or $+1$; the coefficient of a^3x^2 will be $-4 + 4$, or 0, and therefore the term a^3x^2 will not appear in the result.

Exercise 19.

Subtract:

1. $a - 2b + 3c$ from $2a - 3b + 4c$.

2. $a - 3b - 5c$ from $3a - 5b + c$.

3. $2x - 4y + 6z$ from $4x - y - 2z$.

4. $5x - 11y - 3z$ from $6x - 7y + 2z$.

5. $ab - ac - bc + bd$ from $ab + ac + bc + bd$.

6. $3ab + 2ac - 3bc + bd$ from $5ab - ac + bc + bd$.

7. $2x^3 - x^2 - 5x + 3$ from $3x^3 + 2x^2 - 3x - 5$.

8. $7x^2 - 5x + 1 - a$ from $x^3 - x + 1 - a$.

9. $7b^3 + 8c^3 - 15abc$ from $9b^3 + 3abc - 7c^3$.

10. $x^4 + x - 5x^3 + 5$ from $7 - 2x^2 - 3x^3 + x^4$.

11. $a^3 + b^3 + c^3 - 3abc$ from $3abc + a^3 - 2b^3 - 3c^3$.

12. $2x^4 - 5x^2 + 7x - 3$ from $x^4 + 2 - 2x^3 - x^2$.

13. $1 - x^5 - x + x^4 - x^3$ from $x^4 + 1 + x + x^2$.

14. $a^3 - b^3 + 3a^2b - 3ab^2$ from $a^3 + b^3 - a^2b - ab^2$.

15. $a^2b - ab^2 - 3a^3b^3 - b^4$ from $b^4 - 5a^3b^3 - 2ab^2 + a^2b$.

16. $-x^3 + 7x^2y - 2y^3 + 3xy^2$ from $3x^3 + 5y^3 - xy^2 + 4x^2y$.

84. Parentheses or Brackets. We have for positive numbers (§§ 37, 38):

$$a + (b + c) = a + b + c, \qquad \therefore a + b + c = a + (b + c);$$
$$a + (b - c) = a + b - c, \qquad \therefore a + b - c = a + (b - c);$$
$$a - (b + c) = a - b - c, \qquad \therefore a - b - c = a - (b + c);$$
$$a - (b - c) = a - b + c, \qquad \therefore a - b + c = a - (b - c).$$

That is, a parenthesis preceded by + may be removed *without changing the sign of any term within the parenthesis*; and any number of terms may be enclosed within a parenthesis preceded by the sign +, *without changing the sign of any term.*

A parenthesis preceded by the sign − may be removed, *provided the sign of every term within the parenthesis is changed*, namely, + to −, and − to +; and any number of terms may be enclosed within a parenthesis preceded by the sign −, *provided the sign of every term enclosed is changed.*

The same laws hold for *negative numbers.*

85. Expressions may occur having a parenthesis within a parenthesis. In such cases parentheses of different shapes are used, and the beginner when he meets with a branch of a parenthesis (, or bracket [, or brace {, must look carefully for the other part, whatever may intervene; and all that is included between the two parts of each parenthesis must be treated as the sign before it directs, without regard to other parentheses. It is best to remove each parenthesis in succession, *beginning with* *the innermost.*

$$\begin{aligned} a - &\{b - [c - (d - e) + f]\} \\ &= a - \{b - [c - d + e + f]\} \\ &= a - \{b - c + d - e - f\} \\ &= a - b + c - d + e + f. \end{aligned}$$

Exercise 20.

Remove the brackets and collect the like terms:

1. $a - b - (b - c) - a + 2b$.

2. $x - [x - (a - b) + a - y]$.

3. $3x - \{2y - [-7c - 2x] + y\}$.

4. $5a - [7 - (2b + 5) - 2a]$.

5. $x - [2x + (3a - 2x) - 5a]$.

6. $x - [15y - (13z + 12x)]$.

7. $2a - b + [4c - (b + 2c)]$.

8. $5a - \{b + [3c - (2b - c)]\}$.

9. $7x - \{5y - [3z - (3x + z)]\}$.

10. $(a - b + c) - (b - a - c) + (a + b - 2c)$.

11. $3x - [-2y - (2y - 3x) + z] + [x - (y - 2z - x)]$.

12. $x - [2x + (x - 2y) + 2y] - 3x - \{4x - [(x + 2y) - y]\}$.

13. $x - [y + z - x - (x + y) - z] + (3x - \overline{2y + z})$.

NOTE. The expression $-\overline{2y + z}$ is equivalent to $-(2y + z)$.

Consider *all the factors* that precede x, y, and z, respectively, as the *coefficients* of these letters, and collect in brackets the coefficients of each of these letters:

14. $ax + by + cz - ay + az - bx = (a - b)x - (a - b)y + (a + c)z$.

15. $ax + az + by - cz - ay + cx$.

16. $2ax - 3ay - 4by + 5cx - 6bz - 7cz$.

17. $az - bmy + 3cz - anx - cny + acx$.

18. $mnx - x - mny - y + mnz + z$.

CHAPTER V.

MULTIPLICATION AND DIVISION.

Compound Integral Expressions.

86. Multiplication. Polynomials by Monomials.

We have for positive numbers (§ 39),

$$a(b + c) = ab + ac,$$
$$a(b - c) = ab - ac.$$

The same law holds for negative numbers.

To multiply a polynomial by a monomial, therefore,

Multiply each term of the polynomial by the monomial, and add the partial products.

1. Find the product of $ab + ac - bc$ and abc.

$$\begin{array}{r} ab + ac - bc \\ abc \\ \hline a^2b^2c + a^2bc^2 - ab^2c^2 \end{array}$$

Note. We multiply ab, the first term of the multiplicand, by abc, and work to the right.

Exercise 21.

Find the product of:

1. $x + 7$ and x.

2. $2x - 3y$ and $4x$.

3. $2x - 3y$ and $7y$.

4. $x - 2a$ and $2a$.

5. $-x + 3b$ and $-b$.

6. $2a^2 - 3ab$ and $-3a$.

7. $2x^2 + 3xz$ and $5z$.

8. $a^2 - 5ab$ and $5ab$.

9. $x^2 - 3xy$ and $-y^2$.

10. $2x^3 - 3x^2$ and $2x^2$.

11. $x^2 - 3y^2$ and $4y$.

12. $x^2 - 3y^2$ and $-x^2$.

13. $b^3 - a^2b^2$ and $-a^3$.

14. $-a^2b^2 - a^3$ and $-a^2$.

15. $2x^3 - 3x^2 + x$ and $2x^2$.

16. $a^2 - 5ab - b^2$ and $5ab$.

17. $a^3 + 2a^2b + 2ab^2$ and a^2.

18. $a^3 + 2a^2b + 2ab^2$ and b^3.

19. $4x^2 - 6xy - 9y^2$ and $2x$.

20. $-x^2 - 2xy + y^2$ and $-y$.

21. $-a^3 - a^2b^2 - b^3$ and $-a^2$.

22. $-x^2 + 2xy - y^2$ and $-y^2$.

23. $3a^2b^2 - 4ab^3 + a^3b$ and $5a^2b^2$.

24. $-ax^2 + 3axy^2 - ay^4$ and $-3ay^2$.

25. $x^{12} - x^{10}y^3 - x^3y^{10}$ and x^3y^2.

26. $-2x^3 + 3x^2y^2 - 2xy^3$ and $-2x^2y^3$.

27. $a^3x^2y^5 - a^2xy^4 - ay^3$ and $a^7x^3y^5$.

28. $3a^2b^2 - 2ab^3 + 5a^3b$ and $5a^2b^3$.

87. Multiplication. Polynomials by Polynomials.

If we have $m + n + p$ to be multiplied by $a + b + c$, we may substitute M for the multiplier $a + b + c$. Then

$$M(m + n + p) = Mm + Mn + Mp.$$

If now we substitute $a + b + c$ for M, we shall have

$$\begin{aligned}&(a + b + c)m + (a + b + c)n + (a + b + c)p\\ &= am + bm + cm + an + bn + cn + ap + bp + cp\\ &= am + an + ap + bm + bn + bp + cm + cn + cp.\end{aligned}$$

To find the product of two polynomials, therefore,

Multiply every term of the multiplicand by each term of the multiplier, and add the partial products.

88. In multiplying polynomials, it is a convenient arrangement to write the multiplier under the multiplicand, and place like terms of the partial products in columns.

1. Multiply $2x - 3y$ by $5x - 4y$.

$$\begin{array}{rrl}
2x & - & 3\ y \\
5x & - & 4\ y \\
\hline
10x^2 & - & 15\ xy \\
 & - & 8\ xy + 12y^2 \\
\hline
10x^2 & - & 23\ xy + 12y^2
\end{array}$$

We multiply $2x$, the first term of the multiplicand, by $5x$, the first term of the multiplier, and obtain $10x^2$, then $-3y$, the second term of the multiplicand, by $5x$, and obtain $-15xy$. The first line of partial products is $10x^2 - 15xy$. In multiplying by $-4y$, we obtain for a second line of partial products $-8xy+12y^2$, which is put one place to the right, so that the like terms $-15xy$ and $-8xy$ may stand in the same column. We then add the coefficients of the like terms, and obtain the complete product in its simplest form.

2. Multiply $2a + 3 - 4a^2$ by $3 - 2a^2 - 3a$.

Arrange both multiplicand and multiplier according to the *ascending* powers of a.

$$\begin{array}{rrrrr}
3 + 2a & - \ \ 4a^2 & & \\
3 - 3a & - \ \ 2a^2 & & \\
\hline
9 + 6a & - 12a^2 & & \\
- 9a & - \ \ 6a^2 & + 12a^3 & \\
 & - \ \ 6a^2 & - \ \ 4a^3 & + 8a^4 \\
\hline
9 - 3a & - 24a^2 & + \ \ 8a^3 & + 8a^4
\end{array}$$

3. Multiply $3x + x^4 - 2x^2$ by $x^3 - 2 - x$.

Arrange according to the *descending* powers of x.

$$\begin{array}{l}
x^4 - 2x^2 + 3x \\
x^3 - x - 2 \\
\hline
x^7 - 2x^5 + 3x^4 \\
\quad - x^5 \qquad\qquad + 2x^3 - 3x^2 \\
\qquad\qquad - 2x^4 \qquad\qquad + 4x^2 - 6x \\
\hline
x^7 - 3x^5 + x^4 + 2x^3 + x^2 - 6x
\end{array}$$

4. Multiply $a^2 + b^2 + c^2 - ab - bc - ac$ by $a + b + c$.

Arrange according to descending powers of a.

$$\begin{array}{l}
a^2 - ab - ac + b^2 - bc + c^2 \\
a + b + c \\
\hline
a^3 - a^2b - a^2c + ab^2 - abc + ac^2 \\
\quad + a^2b \qquad\qquad - ab^2 - abc \qquad\qquad + b^3 - b^2c + bc^2 \\
\qquad\qquad + a^2c \qquad\qquad - abc - ac^2 \qquad\qquad + b^2c - bc^2 + c^3 \\
\hline
a^3 \qquad\qquad\qquad\qquad - 3abc \qquad\qquad + b^3 \qquad\qquad\qquad + c^3
\end{array}$$

NOTE. The pupil should observe that, with a view to bringing like terms of the partial products in columns, the terms of the multiplicand and multiplier are arranged in the *same order*.

Exercise 22.

Find the product of:

1. $x+7$ and $x+6$.

2. $x-7$ and $x+6$.

3. $x+7$ and $x-6$.

4. $x-7$ and $x-6$.

5. $x+8$ and $x-5$.

6. $2x+3$ and $2x+3$.

7. $2x-3$ and $2x-3$.

8. $2x+3$ and $2x-3$.

9. $3x-2$ and $2-3x$.

10. $5x-3$ and $4x-7$.

11. $a-2b$ and $a+3b$.

12. $a-7b$ and $a-5b$.

13. $5x-3y$ and $5x-3y$.

14. $x-b$ and $x-c$.

15. $2m-p$ and $4m-3p$.

16. $a+b+c$ and $a-c$.

17. a^2-ab+b^2 and a^2+b^2.

18. x^3-3x^2+7 and x^2-3.

19. a^2+ab+b^2 and $a-b$.

20. a^2-ab+b^2 and $a+b$.

21. $x^2+5x-10$ and $2x^2+3x-4$.

22. $3x^3-2x^2+x$ and $3x^2+2x-2$.

23. $x^3+2x^2y+3xy^2$ and $x^2-2xy+y^2$.

24. $a^2-3ab-b^2$ and $-a^2+ab+2b^2$.

25. $3a^2b^2+2ab^3-5a^3b$ and $5a^2b^2-ab^3-b^4$.

26. $a^2-2ab+b^2$ and $a^2+2ab+b^2$.

27. $ab + ac + cd$ and $ab - ac + cd$.

28. $3x^2y^2 + xy^3 - 2x^3y$ and $x^2y^2 + xy^3 - 3y^4$.

29. $x^2 + 2xy - y^2$ and $x^2 - 2xy + y^2$.

30. $3x^2 + xy - y^2$ and $x^2 - 2xy - 3y^2$.

31. $a^2 - 2ab - b^2$ and $b^2 - 2ab - a^2$.

32. $a^2 + b^2 + c^2 - ac$ and $a^2 - b^2 - c^2$.

33. $a^2 + 4abx - 4a^2b^2x^2$ and $a^2 - 4abx + 4a^2b^2x^2$.

34. $3a^2 - 2abx + b^2x^2$ and $2a^2 + 3abx - 2b^2x^2$.

35. $2x^3y + 4x^2y^2 - 8xy^3$ and $2xy^3 - 3x^2y^2 + 5x^3y$.

89. Division. Polynomials by Monomials.

Since $$a(b + c - d) = ab + ac - ad,$$

$$\therefore \frac{ab + ac - ad}{a} = \frac{ab}{a} + \frac{ac}{a} - \frac{ad}{a}$$
$$= b + c - d.$$

To divide a polynomial by a monomial, therefore,

Divide each term of the dividend by the divisor, and add the partial quotients.

Divide $3a^4b^2c - 9a^3bc^2 - 6a^2c^3$ by $3a^2c$.

$$\frac{3a^4b^2c - 9a^3bc^2 - 6a^2c^3}{3a^2c} = \frac{3a^4b^2c}{3a^2c} - \frac{9a^3bc^2}{3a^2c} - \frac{6a^2c^3}{3a^2c}$$
$$= a^2b^2 - 3abc - 2c^2.$$

Exercise 23.

Divide:

1. $2a^3 - a^2$ by a.
2. $42a^5 - 6a^2$ by $6a$.
3. $21x^4 + 3x^2$ by $3x^2$.
4. $35m^4 - 7p^2$ by 7.
5. $27x^5 - 45x^4$ by $9x^2$.
6. $24x^6 - 8x^3$ by $-8x^3$.
7. $34x^3 - 51x^2$ by $17x$.
8. $5x^5 - 10x^3$ by $-5x^3$.
9. $-3a^2 - 6ac$ by $-3a$.
10. $-5x^3 + x^2y$ by $-x^2$.
11. $2a^5x^3 - 2a^4x^2$ by $2a^4x^2$.
12. $-x^2y - x^2y^2$ by $-xy$.
13. $9a - 12b + 6c$ by -3.
14. $a^3b^2 - a^2b^5 - a^4b^2$ by a^2b.
15. $3x^3 - 6x^2y - 9xy^2$ by $3x$.
16. $x^2y^2 - x^3y - xy^3$ by xy.
17. $a^3 - a^2b - ab^2$ by $-a$.
18. $a^2b - ab + ab^2$ by $-ab$.
19. $xy - x^2y^2 + x^3y^3$ by $-xy$.
20. $-x^6 - 2x^5 - x^4$ by $-x^4$.
21. $a^2x - abx - acx$ by ax.
22. $3x^5y^2 - 3x^4y^3 - 3x^2y^4$ by $3x^2y^2$.
23. $a^2b^2 - 2ab - 3ab^3$ by ab.
24. $3a^3c^3 + 3a^2c - 3ac^2$ by $3ac$.

90. Division. Polynomials by Polynomials.

$$
\begin{array}{lcl}
\text{If the divisor (one factor)} & = & a + \;\; b + \;\; c, \\
\text{and the quotient (other factor)} & = & \underline{n + \;\; p + \;\; q,} \\
\text{then the dividend (product)} & = & \begin{cases} \;\;\; an + bn + cn \\ + \; ap + bp + cp \\ + \; aq + bq + cq. \end{cases}
\end{array}
$$

The first term of the dividend is an; that is, the product of a, the first term of the divisor, by n, the first term of the quotient. The first term n of the quotient is therefore found by dividing an, the first term of the dividend, by a, the first term of the divisor.

If the partial product formed by multiplying the entire divisor by n be subtracted from the dividend, the first term of the remainder ap is the product of a, the first term of the divisor, by p, the second term of the quotient; that is, the second term of the quotient is obtained by dividing the first term of the remainder by the first term of the divisor. In like manner, the third term of the quotient is obtained by dividing the first term of the new remainder by the first term of the divisor; and so on.

To divide one polynomial by another, therefore,

Arrange both the dividend and divisor in ascending or descending powers of some common letter.

Divide the first term of the dividend by the first term of the divisor.

Write the result as the first term of the quotient.

Multiply all the terms of the divisor by the first term of the quotient.

Subtract the product from the dividend.

If there is a remainder, consider it as a new dividend, and proceed as before.

91. It is of fundamental importance to arrange the dividend and divisor *in the same order* with respect to a common letter, and *to keep this order throughout the operation.*

The beginner should study carefully the processes in the following examples:

1. Divide $x^2 + 18x + 77$ by $x + 7$.

$$\begin{array}{r|l} x^2 + 18x + 77 & x+7 \\ \cline{2-2} x^2 + 7x & x+11 \\ \hline 11x + 77 & \\ 11x + 77 & \\ \cline{1-1} \end{array}$$

NOTE. The pupil will notice that by this process we have in effect separated the dividend into two parts, $x^2 + 7x$ and $11x + 77$, and divided each part by $x + 7$, and that the complete quotient is the sum of the partial quotients x and 11. Thus,

$$x^2 + 18x + 77 = x^2 + 7x + 11x + 77 = (x^2 + 7x) + (11x + 77).$$

$$\therefore \frac{x^2 + 18x + 77}{x+7} = \frac{x^2 + 7x}{x+7} + \frac{11x + 77}{x+7} = x + 11.$$

2. Divide $a^2 - 2ab + b^2$ by $a - b$.

$$\begin{array}{l|l}
a^2 - 2ab + b^2 & a - b \\ \cline{2-2}
a^2 - ab & a - b \\ \cline{1-1}
\quad - ab + b^2 & \\
\quad - ab + b^2 & \\ \cline{1-1}
\end{array}$$

3. Divide $a^4 - ab^3 + b^4 + 2a^2b^2 - a^3b$ by $a^2 + b^2$.

Arrange according to the descending powers of a.

$$\begin{array}{l|l}
a^4 - a^3b + 2a^2b^2 - ab^3 + b^4 & a^2 + b^2 \\ \cline{2-2}
a^4 \qquad\quad + a^2b^2 & a^2 - ab + b^2 \\ \cline{1-1}
\quad - a^3b + a^2b^2 - ab^3 + b^4 & \\
\quad - a^3b \qquad\quad - ab^3 & \\ \cline{1-1}
\qquad\qquad + a^2b^2 \qquad + b^4 & \\
\qquad\qquad + a^2b^2 \qquad + b^4 & \\ \cline{1-1}
\end{array}$$

4. Divide $10a^2b^2 - 20b^4 - 17a^3b + 6a^4 + ab^3$ by $2a^2 - 4b^2 - 3ab$.

Arrange according to descending powers of a.

$$\begin{array}{l|l}
6a^4 - 17a^3b + 10a^2b^2 + ab^3 - 20b^4 & 2a^2 - 3ab - 4b^2 \\ \cline{2-2}
6a^4 - 9a^3b - 12a^2b^2 & 3a^2 - 4ab + 5b^2 \\ \cline{1-1}
\quad - 8a^3b + 22a^2b^2 + ab^3 - 20b^4 & \\
\quad - 8a^3b + 12a^2b^2 + 16ab^3 & \\ \cline{1-1}
\qquad\qquad 10a^2b^2 - 15ab^3 - 20b^4 & \\
\qquad\qquad 10a^2b^2 - 15ab^3 - 20b^4 & \\ \cline{1-1}
\end{array}$$

5. Divide $5x^3 - 3x^4 - 4x^2 + 1 + x$ by $1 + 2x - 3x^2$.

Arrange according to ascending powers of x.

$$
\begin{array}{r|l}
1 + x - 4x^2 + 5x^3 - 3x^4 & 1 + 2x - 3x^2 \\ \cline{2-2}
1 + 2x - 3x^2 \phantom{{}+ 5x^3 - 3x^4} & 1 - x + x^2 \\ \cline{1-1}
- x - x^2 + 5x^3 - 3x^4 & \\
- x - 2x^2 + 3x^3 \phantom{{}- 3x^4} & \\ \cline{1-1}
x^2 + 2x^3 - 3x^4 & \\
x^2 + 2x^3 - 3x^4 &
\end{array}
$$

6. Divide $a^3 + b^3 + c^3 - 3abc$ by $a + b + c$.

Arrange according to descending powers of a.

$$
\begin{array}{r|l}
a^3 \qquad\qquad - 3abc \qquad\qquad + b^3 + c^3 & a + b + c \\ \cline{2-2}
a^3 + a^2b + a^2c \phantom{{} - 3abc \qquad\qquad + b^3 + c^3} & a^2 - ab - ac \\ \cline{1-1}
- a^2b - a^2c - 3abc \qquad\qquad + b^3 + c^3 & \quad + b^2 - bc + c^2 \\
- a^2b - ab^2 - abc & \\ \cline{1-1}
- a^2c + ab^2 - 2abc \qquad\qquad + b^3 + c^3 & \\
- a^2c \qquad\quad - abc - ac^2 \phantom{{} + b^3 + c^3} & \\ \cline{1-1}
ab^2 - abc + ac^2 + b^3 + c^3 & \\
ab^2 \qquad\qquad\qquad + b^3 + b^2c & \\ \cline{1-1}
- abc + ac^2 - b^2c + c^3 & \\
- abc \qquad\quad - b^2c - bc^2 & \\ \cline{1-1}
ac^2 + bc^2 + c^3 & \\
ac^2 + bc^2 + c^3 & \\ \cline{1-1}
\end{array}
$$

Exercise 24.

Divide:

1. $x^2 + 15x + 56$ by $x + 7$.

2. $x^2 - 15x + 56$ by $x - 7$.

3. $x^2 + x - 56$ by $x - 7$.

4. $x^2 - x - 56$ by $x + 7$.

5. $2a^2 + 11a + 5$ by $2a + 1$.

6. $6a^2 - 7a - 3$ by $2a - 3$.

7. $4a^2 + 23a + 15$ by $4a + 3$.

8. $3a^2 - 4a - 4$ by $2 - a$.

9. $x^4 + x^2 + 1$ by $x^2 + x + 1$.

10. $x^8 + x^4 + 1$ by $x^4 - x^2 + 1$.

11. $1 - a^3b^3$ by $1 - ab$.

12. $x^3 - 8x - 3$ by $x - 3$.

13. $a^2 - 2ab + b^2 - c^2$ by $a - b - c$.

14. $a^2 + 2ab + b^2 - c^2$ by $a + b + c$.

15. $x^2 - y^2 + 2yz - z^2$ by $x - y + z$.

16. $c^4 + 2c^2 - c + 2$ by $c^2 - c + 1$.

17. $x^2 - 4y^2 - 4yz - z^2$ by $x + 2y + z$.

Arrange and divide:

18. $x^3 - 6a^3 + 11a^2x - 6ax^2$ by $x^2 + 6a^2 - 5ax$.

19. $a^2 - 4b^2 - 9c^2 + 12bc$ by $a - 3c + 2b$.

20. $2a^3 - 8a + a^4 + 12 - 7a^2$ by $2 + a^2 - 3a$.

21. $q^4 + 6q^3 + 4 + 12q + 13q^2$ by $3q + 2 + q^2$.

22. $27a^3 - 8b^3$ by $3a - 2b$.

Find the remainder when:

23. $a^4 + 9a^2 + 15 - 11a - 7a^3$ is divided by $a - 5$.

24. $7 - 8c^2 + 5c^3 + 8c$ is divided by $5c - 3$.

25. $3 + 11a^3 + 30a^4 - 82a^2 - 5a$ is divided by $3a^2 - 4 + 2a$.

26. $2x^3 - 16x + 10 - 39x^2 + 17x^4$ is divided by $2 - 5x^2 - 4x$.

Exercise 25.

Miscellaneous Examples.

1. Add $2a^2 - 3ac - 3ab$; $2b^2 + 3ac + a^2$; $-a^2 - 2b^2 + 3ab$.

2. Subtract $3a^4 - 2a^3b + 4a^2b^2$ from $4b^4 - 2ab^3 + 4a^2b^2$.

3. Simplify $x - y - \{z - x - (y - x + z)\}$.

4. Multiply $a^2 + b^2 + c^2 - d^2$ by $a^2 + b^2 - c^2 + d^2$.

5. Divide $10y^6 + 2 - 12y^5$ by $1 + y^2 - 2y$.

6. If $a = 1$, $b = 2$, and $c = -3$, find the value of $a^2 + b^2 + c^2 + 2ab + 2ac + 2bc$.

7. Simplify $x - (y - z) - \{4y + [2y - (z - x)]\}$.

8. Multiply $a^2 + b^2 + c^2 - ab - ac - bc$ by $a + b + c$.

9. Divide $16y^4 - 21x^2y^2 + 21x^3y - 10x^4$ by $4y^2 - 5x^2 + 3xy$.

10. Add $-2a^4 + 3a^3b - 4a^2b^2$; $2a^3b - 3a^2b^2$; $7a^2b^2 + 2a^4 - b^4$.

11. From $3x^3 + 5x - 1$ take the sum of $x - 5 + 5x^2$ and $3 + 4x - 3x^2$.

12. The minuend is $9c^2 + 11c - 5$, and the remainder is $6c^2 - 13c + 7$. What is the subtrahend?

13. Find the remainder when $a^4 + 6b^4$ is divided by $a^2 + 2ab + 2b^2$.

14. Multiply $2 - 5x^2 - 4x$ by $5 + 2x - 3x^2$.

15. Divide $a^6 + a^5x + a^4x^2 - a^3x^3 + x^6$ by $a^2 + ax + x^2$.

Bracket the coefficients of the different powers of x:

16. $ax^3 - cx + bx^2 - bx^3 + cx^2 - x$.

17. $ax^4 - 2x + bx^4 - cx - ax^3 + bx^3$.

18. $x^3 - bx^2 - cx + bx - cx^2 + ax^3$.

CHAPTER VI.

MULTIPLICATION AND DIVISION.

Special Rules.

92. Special Rules of Multiplication. Some results of multiplication are of so great utility in shortening algebraic work that they should be carefully noticed and remembered. The following are important:

93. Square of the Sum of Two Numbers.

$$\begin{aligned}(a+b)^2 &= (a+b)(a+b)\\ &= a(a+b)+b(a+b)\\ &= a^2+ab+ab+b^2\\ &= a^2+2ab+b^2.\end{aligned}$$

Since a and b stand for any two numbers, we have

Rule 1. *The square of the sum of two numbers is the sum of their squares plus twice their product.*

94. Square of the Difference of Two Numbers.

$$\begin{aligned}(a-b)^2 &= (a-b)(a-b)\\ &= a(a-b)-b(a-b)\\ &= a^2-ab-ab+b^2\\ &= a^2-2ab+b^2.\end{aligned}$$

Hence we have

RULE 2. *The square of the difference of two numbers is the sum of their squares minus twice their product.*

95. Product of the Sum and Difference of Two Numbers.

$$\begin{aligned}(a+b)(a-b) &= a(a-b)+b(a-b)\\ &= a^2-ab+ab-b^2\\ &= a^2-b^2.\end{aligned}$$

Hence, we have

RULE 3. *The product of the sum and difference of two numbers is the difference of their squares.*

If we put $2x$ for a, and 3 for b, we have

Rule 1, $(2x+3)^2 = 4x^2+12x+9.$

Rule 2, $(2x-3)^2 = 4x^2-12x+9.$

Rule 3, $(2x+3)(2x-3) = 4x^2-9.$

Exercise 26.

Write by inspection the value of:

1. $(m+n)^2.$

2. $(c-a)^2.$

3. $(a+2c)^2.$

4. $(3a-2b)^2.$

5. $(2a + 3b)^2$.

6. $(a - 3b)^2$.

7. $(2x - y)^2$.

8. $(y - 2x)^2$.

9. $(a + 5b)^2$.

10. $(2a - 5c)^2$.

11. $(x + y)(x - y)$.

12. $(4a - b)(4a + b)$.

13. $(2b - 3c)(2b + 3c)$.

14. $(x + 5b)(x + 5b)$.

15. $(y - 2z)(y - 2z)$.

16. $(y + 3z)(y - 3z)$.

17. $(2a - 3b)(2a + 3b)$.

18. $(2a - 3b)(2a - 3b)$.

19. $(2a + 3b)(2a + 3b)$.

20. $(5x + 3a)(5x - 3a)$.

96. Product of Two Binomials of the Form $x+a$, $x+b$. The product of two binomials which have the form $x + a$, $x + b$, should be carefully noticed and remembered.

1.
$$\begin{aligned}(x+5)(x+3) &= x(x+3) + 5(x+3)\\ &= x^2 + 3x + 5x + 15\\ &= x^2 + 8x + 15.\end{aligned}$$

2.
$$\begin{aligned}(x-5)(x-3) &= x(x-3) - 5(x-3)\\ &= x^2 - 3x - 5x + 15\\ &= x^2 - 8x + 15.\end{aligned}$$

3.
$$\begin{aligned}(x+5)(x-3) &= x(x-3) + 5(x-3)\\ &= x^2 - 3x + 5x - 15\\ &= x^2 + 2x - 15.\end{aligned}$$

4.
$$\begin{aligned}(x-5)(x+3) &= x(x+3)-5(x+3)\\ &= x^2+3x-5x-15\\ &= x^2-2x-15.\end{aligned}$$

1. Each of these results has three terms.

2. The first term of each result is the product of the first terms of the binomials.

3. The last term of each result is the product of the second terms of the binomials.

4. The middle term of each result has for a coefficient the *algebraic sum* of the second terms of the binomials.

97. The intermediate step given above may be omitted, and the products written at once by *inspection*. Thus,

1. Multiply $x+8$ by $x+7$.

$$8+7=15,\quad 8\times 7=56.$$
$$\therefore (x+8)(x+7)=x^2+15x+56.$$

2. Multiply $x-8$ by $x-7$.

$$(-8)+(-7)=-15,\quad (-8)(-7)=+56.$$
$$\therefore (x-8)(x-7)=x^2-15x+56.$$

3. Multiply $x - 7y$ by $x + 6y$.

$$-7 + 6 = -1, \quad (-7) \times 6y = -42y^2.$$
$$\therefore (x - 7y)(x + 6y) = x^2 - xy - 42y^2.$$

4. Multiply $x + 6y$ by $x - 5y$.

$$+6 - 5 = 1, \quad 6y \times (-5y) = -30y^2.$$
$$\therefore (x + 6y)(x - 5y) = x^2 + xy - 30y^2.$$

Exercise 27.

Write by inspection the product of:

1. $(x + 7)(x + 4)$.

2. $(x - 3)(x + 7)$.

3. $(x - 2)(x - 4)$.

4. $(x - 6)(x - 10)$.

5. $(x + 7)(x - 4)$.

6. $(x + a)(x - 2a)$.

7. $(x + 3a)(x - a)$.

8. $(a + 3c)(a + 3c)$.

9. $(a + 2x)(a - 4x)$.

10. $(a - 3b)(a - 4b)$.

11. $(a^2 - c)(a^2 + 2c)$.

12. $(x - 17)(x - 3)$.

13. $(x + 6y)(x - 5y)$.

14. $(3 + 2x)(3 - x)$.

15. $(5 + 2x)(1 - 2x)$.

16. $(a - 2b)(a + 3b)$.

17. $(a^2b^2 - x^2)(a^2b^2 - 5x^2)$.

18. $(a^3b - ab^3)(a^3b + 5ab^3)$.

19. $(x^2y - xy^2)(x^2y - 3xy^2)$.

20. $(x^2y + xy^2)(x^2y + xy^2)$.

21. $(x+a)(x+b)$.

22. $(x+a)(x-b)$.

23. $(x-a)(x+b)$.

24. $(x-a)(x-b)$.

25. $(x+2a)(x+2b)$.

26. $(x-2a)(x+2b)$.

27. $(x+2a)(x-2b)$.

28. $(x-2a)(x-2b)$.

29. $(x-a)(x+3a)$.

30. $(x-2a)(x+3a)$.

98. Special Rules of Division. Some results in division are so important in abridging algebraic work that they should be carefully noticed and remembered.

99. Difference of Two Squares.

Since $(a+b)(a-b)=a^2-b^2$,

$$\therefore \frac{a^2-b^2}{a+b}=a-b; \quad \text{and} \quad \frac{a^2-b^2}{a-b}=a+b. \quad \text{Hence,}$$

RULE 1. *The difference of the squares of two numbers is divisible by the sum, and by the difference, of the numbers.*

Exercise 28.

Write by inspection the quotient of:

1. $\dfrac{x^2-4}{x-2}$.

2. $\dfrac{x^2-4}{x+2}$.

3. $\dfrac{a^2-9}{a-3}$.

4. $\dfrac{a^2-9}{a+3}$.

5. $\dfrac{c^2-25}{c-5}$.

6. $\dfrac{c^2-25}{c+5}$.

7. $\dfrac{49x^2-y^2}{7x-y}$.

8. $\dfrac{49x^2-y^2}{7x+y}$.

9. $\dfrac{9b^2-1}{3b-1}$.

10. $\dfrac{9b^2-1}{3b+1}$.

11. $\dfrac{16x^4-25a^2}{4x^2-5a}$.

12. $\dfrac{16x^4-25a^2}{4x^2+5a}$.

13. $\dfrac{9x^2-25y^2}{3x-5y}$.

14. $\dfrac{a^2-(b-c)^2}{a-(b-c)}$.

15. $\dfrac{a^2-(b-c)^2}{a+(b-c)}$.

16. $\dfrac{a^2-(2b-c)^2}{a-(2b-c)}$.

17. $\dfrac{(5a-7b)^2-1}{(5a-7b)-1}$.

18. $\dfrac{(5a-7b)^2-1}{(5a-7b)+1}$.

19. $\dfrac{z^2-(x-y)^2}{z-(x-y)}$.

20. $\dfrac{z^2-(x-y)^2}{z+(x-y)}$.

21. $\dfrac{a^2-(2b-c)^2}{a+(2b-c)}$.

22. $\dfrac{(x+3y)^2-z^2}{(x+3y)-z}$.

23. $\dfrac{(x+3y)^2-z^2}{x+3y+z}$.

24. $\dfrac{(a+2b)^2-4c^2}{(a+2b)-2c}$.

25. $\dfrac{(a+2b)^2-4c^2}{(a+2b)+2c}$.

26. $\dfrac{1-(3x-2y)^2}{1+(3x-2y)}$.

100. Difference of Two Cubes. By performing the division we have

$$\frac{a^3 - b^3}{a - b} = a^2 + ab + b^2. \quad \text{Hence,}$$

RULE 2. *The difference of the cubes of two numbers is divisible by the difference of the numbers, and the quotient is the sum of the squares of the numbers plus their product.*

Exercise 29.

Write by inspection the quotient of:

1. $\frac{1 - x^3}{1 - x}$.
2. $\frac{1 - 8a^3}{1 - 2a}$.
3. $\frac{1 - 27c^3}{1 - 2c}$.
4. $\frac{8a^3 - b^3}{2a - b}$.
5. $\frac{64b^3 - 27c^3}{4b - 3c}$.
6. $\frac{27x^3 - 8y^3}{3x - 2y}$.
7. $\frac{x^3y^3 - z^3}{xy - z}$.
8. $\frac{a^3b^3 - 8}{ab - 2}$.
9. $\frac{125a^3 - b^3}{5a - b}$.
10. $\frac{a^3 - 8b^3}{a - 2b}$.
11. $\frac{a^3 - 64}{a - 4}$.
12. $\frac{a^9 - 27}{a^3 - 3}$.
13. $\frac{a^{12} - x^6y^6}{a^4 - x^2y^2}$.
14. $\frac{x^{15} - a^9b^9}{x^5 - a^3b^3}$.
15. $\frac{27x^3y^3 - z^{12}}{3xy - z^4}$.
16. $\frac{x^3y^3z^3 - 1}{xyz - 1}$.
17. $\frac{8a^3b^3c^3 - 27}{2abc - 3}$.
18. $\frac{1 - 64x^3y^3z^3}{1 - 4xyz}$.

101. Sum of Two Cubes. By performing the division, we find that

$$\frac{a^3+b^3}{a+b} = a^2 - ab + b^2. \quad \text{Hence,}$$

RULE 3. *The sum of the cubes of two numbers is divisible by the sum of the numbers, and the quotient is the sum of the squares of the numbers minus their product.*

Exercise 30.

Write by inspection the quotient of:

1. $\frac{1+x^3}{1+x}$.
2. $\frac{1+8a^3}{1+2a}$.
3. $\frac{1+27c^3}{1+3c}$.
4. $\frac{8a^3+b^3}{2a+b}$.
5. $\frac{64b^3+27c^3}{4b+3c}$.
6. $\frac{27x^3+8y^3}{3x+2y}$.
7. $\frac{8x^3+125y^3}{2x+5y}$.
8. $\frac{x^3y^3+z^3}{xy+z}$.
9. $\frac{a^3b^3+8}{ab+2}$.
10. $\frac{125a^3+b^3}{5a+b}$.
11. $\frac{a^3+8b^3}{a+2b}$.
12. $\frac{a^6+64}{a^2+4}$.
13. $\frac{a^9+27}{a^3+3}$.
14. $\frac{8a^6+b^3}{2a^2+b}$.
15. $\frac{a^{12}+x^6y^6}{a^4+x^2y^2}$.
16. $\frac{x^{15}+a^9b^9}{x^5+a^3b^3}$.
17. $\frac{27x^3y^3+z^{12}}{3xy+z^4}$.
18. $\frac{x^3y^3z^3+1}{xyz+1}$.
19. $\frac{8a^3b^3c^3+27}{2abc+3}$.
20. $\frac{1+64x^3y^3z^3}{1+4xyz}$.
21. $\frac{1+27a^6b^3c^3}{1+3a^2bc}$.

Find by division the quotient of:

22. $\dfrac{x^4 - y^4}{x - y}$.

23. $\dfrac{x^4 - y^4}{x + y}$.

24. $\dfrac{x^5 - y^5}{x - y}$.

25. $\dfrac{x^5 + y^5}{x + y}$.

26. $\dfrac{x^6 - y^6}{x - y}$.

27. $\dfrac{x^6 - y^6}{x + y}$.

CHAPTER VII.

FACTORS.

102. Rational Expressions. An expression is *rational* when none of its terms contain square or other roots.

103. Factors of Rational and Integral Expressions. By factors of a given integral number in arithmetic we mean integral numbers that will divide the given number without remainder. Likewise by factors of a rational and integral expression in algebra we mean rational and integral expressions that will divide the given expression without remainder.

104. Factors of Monomials. The factors of a monomial may be found by inspection. Thus, the factors of $21a^2b$ are 3, 7, a, a, and b.

105. Factors of Polynomials. The form of a polynomial that can be resolved into factors often suggests the process of finding the factors.

Case I.

106. When all the terms have a common factor.

1. Resolve into factors $3a^2 - 6ab$.

Since $3a$ is seen to be a factor of each term, we have

$$\frac{3a^2 - 6ab}{3a} = \frac{3a^2}{3a} - \frac{6ab}{3a} = a - 2b.$$
$$\therefore\ 3a^2 - 6ab = 3a(a - 2b).$$

Hence, the required factors are $3a$ and $a - 2b$.

2. Resolve into factors $4x^3 + 12x^2 - 8x$.

Since $4x$ is seen to be a factor of each term, we have

$$\frac{4x^3 + 12x^2 - 8x}{4x} = \frac{4x^3}{4x} + \frac{12x^2}{4x} - \frac{8x}{4x}$$
$$= x^2 + 3x - 2.$$
$$\therefore\ 4x^3 + 12x^2 - 8x = 4x(x^2 + 3x - 2).$$

Hence the required factors are $4x$ and $x^2 + 3x - 2$.

Exercise 31.

Resolve into two factors:

1. $2x^2 - 4x$.

2. $3a^3 - 6a$.

3. $5a^2b^2 - 10a^3b^3$.

4. $3x^2y + 4xy^2$.

5. $8a^3b^2 + 4a^2b^3$.

6. $3a^4 - 12a^2 - 6a^3$.

7. $4x^2 - 8x^4 - 12x^5$.

8. $5 - 10x^2y^2 + 15x^2y$.

9. $7a^2 + 14a - 21a^3$.

10. $3x^3y^3 - 6x^4y^4 - 9x^2y^2$.

CASE II.

107. When the terms can be grouped so as to show a common factor in each group.

1. Resolve into factors $ac + ad + bc + bd$.

$$\begin{aligned} ac + ad + bc + bd &= (ac + ad) + (bc + bd) & (1)\\ &= a(c + d) + b(c + d) & (2)\\ &= (a + b)(c + d). & (3) \end{aligned}$$

NOTE. The first two terms of $ac + ad + bc + bd$ are seen to have the common factor a, and the last two terms, the common factor b. Hence we bracket the first two terms and also the last two terms. Then we take out the factor a from $(ac + ad)$ and b from $(bc + bd)$, and get equation (2). Since one factor is seen in (2) to be $c + d$, dividing by $c + d$, we obtain the other factor, $a + b$.

2. Find the factors of $ac + ad - bc - bd$.

$$\begin{aligned} ac + ad - bc - bd &= (ac + ad) - (bc + bd)\\ &= a(c + d) - b(c + d)\\ &= (a - b)(c + d). \end{aligned}$$

NOTE. Here the last two terms, $-bc - bd$, being put within a parenthesis preceded by the sign $-$, have their signs changed to $+$.

3. Resolve into factors $2x^3 - 3x^2 - 4x + 6$.

$$\begin{aligned} 2x^3 - 3x^2 - 4x + 6 &= (2x^3 - 3x^2) - (4x - 6)\\ &= x^2(2x - 3) - 2(2x - 3)\\ &= (x^2 - 2)(2x - 3). \end{aligned}$$

4. Resolve into factors $x^3 + x^2 - ax - a$.

$$\begin{aligned} x^3 + x^2 - ax - a &= (x^3 + x^2) - (ax + a) \\ &= x^2(x + 1) - a(x + 1) \\ &= (x^2 - a)(x + 1). \end{aligned}$$

5. Resolve into factors $x^3 + 3ax^2 + x + 3a$.

$$\begin{aligned} x^3 + 3ax^2 + x + 3a &= (x^3 + 3ax^2) + (x + 3a) \\ &= x^2(x + 3a) + 1(x + 3a) \\ &= (x^2 + 1)(x + 3a). \end{aligned}$$

Exercise 32.

Resolve into factors:

1. $x^3 + x^2 + x + 1$.

2. $x^3 - x^2 + x - 1$.

3. $x^2 + xy + xz + yz$.

4. $ax - bx - ay + by$.

5. $a^2 - ac + ab - bc$.

6. $x^2 - bx + 3x - 3b$.

7. $2x^3 - x^2 + 4x - 2$.

8. $a^2 - 3a - ab + 3b$.

9. $6a^2 + 2ab - 3ac - bc$.

10. $abxy + cxy + abc + c^2$.

11. $ax - ay - bx + cy - cx + by$.

12. $(a - b)^2 - 2c(a - b)$.

Case III.

108. When a binomial is the difference of two squares.

1. Resolve into factors $x^2 - y^2$.

Since, $$(x+y)(x-y) = x^2 - y^2,$$

the factors of $x^2 - y^2$ are $x + y$ and $x - y$.

To find the factors of a binomial when it is the difference of two squares, therefore,

Take the square root of the first term and the square root of the second term.

The sum of these roots will form the first factor;

The difference of these roots will form the second factor.

109. The **square root** of a *monomial* is one of the **two equal factors** of the monomial.

Thus $9x^8y^2 = 3x^4y \times 3x^4y$; and $3x^4y$ is the square root of $9x^8y^2$.

The rule for extracting the square root of a *monomial, when a perfect square*, is as follows:

Extract the square root of the coefficient, and divide the index of each letter by 2.

Exercise 33.

Resolve into factors:

1. $4 - x^2$.
2. $9 - x^2$.
3. $9a^2 - x^2$.
4. $25 - x^2$.
5. $25x^2 - a^2$.
6. $16a^4 - 121$.
7. $121a^4 - 16$.
8. $4a^2b^2 - c^2d^2$.
9. $1 - x^2y^2$.
10. $81x^2y^2 - 1$.
11. $49a^2b^2 - 4$.
12. $25a^4b^4 - 9$.
13. $9a^8b^6 - 16x^{10}$.
14. $144x^2y^2 - 1$.
15. $100x^6y^2z^4 - 1$.
16. $1 - 121a^4b^8c^{12}$.
17. $25a^2 - 64x^6y^6$.
18. $16x^{16} - 25y^{18}$.

Find, by resolving into factors, the value of:

19. $(375)^2 - (225)^2$.
20. $(579)^2 - (559)^2$.
21. $(873)^2 - (173)^2$.
22. $(101)^2 - (99)^2$.
23. $(7244)^2 - (7242)^2$.
24. $(3781)^2 - (219)^2$.

110. If the squares are compound expressions, the same method may be employed.

1. Resolve into factors $(x + 3y)^2 - 16a^2$.

The square root of the first term is $x + 3y$.

The square root of the second term is $4a$.

The sum of these roots is $x + 3y - 4a$.

The difference of these roots is $x + 3y - 4a$.

Therefore $(x + 3y)^2 - 16a^2 = (x + 3y + 4a)(x + 3y - 4a)$.

2. Resolve into factors $a^2 - (3b - 5c)^2$.

The square roots of the terms are a and $(3b - 5c)$.

The sum of these roots is $a + (3b - 5c)$, or $a + 3b - 5c$.

The difference of these roots is $a - (3b - 5c)$, or $a - 3b + 5c$.

Therefore $a^2 - (3b - 5c)^2 = (a + 3b - 5c)(a - 3b + 5c)$.

Exercise 34.

Resolve into factors:

1. $(x + y)^2 - z^2$.

2. $(x - y)^2 - z^2$.

3. $z^2 - (x + y)^2$.

4. $z^2 - (x - y)^2$.

5. $(x + y)^2 - 4z^2$.

6. $4z^2 - (x - y)^2$.

7. $(a + 2b)^2 - c^2$.

8. $(a - 2b)^2 - c^2$.

9. $c^2 - (a - 2b)^2$.

10. $(2a + 5c)^2 - 1$.

11. $1 - (2a - 5c)^2$.

12. $(a + 3b)^2 - 16c^2$.

13. $(a - 5b)^2 - 9c^2$.

14. $16c^2 - (a - 5b)^2$.

15. $4a^2 - (x + y)^2$.

16. $b^2 - (a - 2x)^2$.

17. $4z^2 - (x + 3y)^2$.

18. $9 - (3a - 7b)^2$.

19. $16a^2 - (2b + 5c)^2$.

20. $25c^2 - (3a - 2x)^2$.

21. $9a^2 - (3b - 5c)^2$.

22. $16y^2 - (a - 3c)^2$.

23. $49m^2 - (p + 2q)^2$.

24. $36n^2 - (d - 2c)^2$.

25. $(x + y)^2 - (a + b)^2$.

26. $(x - y)^2 - (a - b)^2$.

27. $(2x + 3)^2 - (2a + b)^2$.

28. $(b - c)^2 - (a - 2x)^2$.

29. $(3x - y)^2 - (2a - b)^2$.

30. $(x - 3y)^2 - (a + 2b)^2$.

31. $(x + 2y)^2 - (a + 3b)^2$.

32. $(x + y)^2 - (a - z)^2$.

Case IV.

111. When a binomial is the difference of two cubes.

Since
$$\frac{a^3 - b^3}{a - b} = a^2 + ab + b^2,$$
the factors of $a^3 - b^3$ are $a - b$ and $a^2 + ab + b^2$.

In like manner we can resolve into factors any expression which can be written as the difference of two cubes.

112. The rule for extracting the cube root of a *monomial, when the monomial is a perfect cube*, is,

Extract the cube root of the coefficient, and divide the index of each letter by 3.

1. Resolve into factors $8a^3 - 27b^6$.

Since $8a^3 = (2a)^3$, and $27b^6 = (3b^2)^3$, we can write $8a^3 - 27b^6$ as $(2a)^3 - (3b^2)^3$.

Since $$a^3 - b^3 = (a - b)(a^2 + ab + b^2),$$

we have, by putting $2a$ for a and $3b^2$ for b,

$$\begin{aligned}(2a)^3 - (3b^2)^3 &= (2a - 3b^2)[(2a)^2 + 2a \times 3b^2 + (3b^2)^2] \\ &= (2a - 3b^2)(4a^2 + 6ab^2 + 9b^4).\end{aligned}$$

2. Resolve into factors $64x^3 - 1$.

$$\begin{aligned}64x^3 - 1 &= (4x)^3 - 1 \\ &= (4x - 1)[(4x)^2 + 4x + 1] \\ &= (4x - 1)(16x^2 + 4x + 1).\end{aligned}$$

To find the factors of a binomial when it is the difference of two cubes, therefore,

Take the difference of the cube roots of the terms for one factor, and the sum of the squares of the cube roots of the terms plus their product for the other factor.

Exercise 35.

Resolve into factors:

1. $8x^3 - y^3$.	**7.** $a^3b^3 - 27c^3$.	**13.** $64x^3 - 729y^3$.
2. $x^3 - 1$.	**8.** $x^3y^3z^3 - 8$.	**14.** $27a^3 - 512c^3$.
3. $x^3y^3 - z^3$.	**9.** $8a^3b^3 - 27y^6$.	**15.** $8x^6 - 125y^3$.
4. $x^3 - 64$.	**10.** $64x^3 - y^9$.	**16.** $64x^{12} - 27y^{15}$.
5. $125a^3 - b^3$.	**11.** $27a^3 - 64c^6$.	**17.** $216 - 8a^3$.
6. $a^3 - 343$.	**12.** $x^3y^3 - 216z^3$.	**18.** $343 - 27y^3$.

Case V.

113. When a binomial is the sum of two cubes.

Since $$\frac{a^3 + b^3}{a + b} = a^2 - ab + b^2,$$

the factors of $a^3 + b^3$ are $a + b$ and $a^2 - ab + b^2$.

In like manner we can resolve into factors any expression which can be written as the sum of two cubes.

1. Resolve into factors $8x^3 + 27y^3$.

Since by § 112, $8x^3 = (2x)^3$ and $27y^3 = (3y)^3$, we can write $8x^3 + 27y^3$ as $(2x)^3 + (3y)^3$.

Since $$a^3 + b^3 = (a + b)(a^2 - ab + b^2),$$

we have, by putting $2x$ for a, and $3y$ for b,

$$\begin{aligned}(2x)^3 + (3y)^3 &= (2x + 3y)[(2x)^2 - 2x \times 3y + (3y)^2] \\ &= (2x + 3y)(4x^2 - 6xy + 9y^2).\end{aligned}$$

2. Resolve into factors $125a^3 + 64x^6$.

$$\begin{aligned}125a^3 &= (5a)^3, \quad 64x^6 = (4x^2)^3; \\ \therefore 125a^3 + 64x^6 &= (5a + 4x^2)[(5a)^2 - 5a \times 4x^2 + (4x^2)^2] \\ &= (5a + 4x^2)(25a^2 - 20ax^2 + 16x^4)\end{aligned}$$

To find the factors of a binomial when it is the sum of two cubes, therefore,

Take the sum of the cube roots of the terms for one factor, and the sum of the squares of the cube roots of the terms minus their product for the other factor.

Exercise 36.

Resolve into factors:

1. $x^3 + 1$.

2. $8x^3 + y^3$.

3. $x^3 + 125$.

4. $64a^3 + 27$.

5. $x^3y^3 + z^3$.

6. $a^3 + 64$.

7. $8a^6 + b^3$.

8. $x^3 + 343$.

9. $8 + x^3y^3z^3$.

10. $y^9 + 64x^3$.

11. $a^3b^3 + 27x^3$.

12. $8y^3z^3 + x^6$.

13. $y^9 + 64x^6$.

14. $64a^{12} + x^{15}$.

15. $27x^{15} + 8a^6$.

16. $27x^9 + 512$.

17. $343 + 64x^3$.

18. $125 + 27y^3$.

Case VI.

114. When a trinomial is a perfect square.

Since $$(x+y)^2 = x^2 + 2xy + y^2,$$
the factors of $x^2 + 2xy + y^2$ are $x + y$ and $x + y$.

Since $$(x-y)^2 = x^2 - 2xy + y^2,$$
the factors of $x^2 - 2xy + y^2$ are $x - y$ and $x - y$.

Therefore, a trinomial is a perfect square, if its first and last terms are perfect squares and positive, and its middle term is twice the product of their square roots.

To find the factors of a trinomial when it is a perfect square, therefore,

Extract the square roots of the first and last terms, and connect these square roots by the sign of the middle term.

Thus, if we wish to find the square root of

$$16a^2 - 24ab + 9b^2,$$

we take the square roots of $16a^2$ and $9b^2$, which are $4a$ and $3b$, respectively, and connect these square roots by the minus sign, the sign of the middle term. The square root is therefore

$$4a - 3b.$$

Again, if we wish to find the square root of

$$25x^2 + 40xy + 16y^2,$$

we take the square roots of $25x^2$ and $16y^2$ and connect these roots by the plus sign, the sign of the middle term. The square root is therefore

$$5x + 4y.$$

Exercise 37.

Resolve into factors:

1. $4x^2 + 4xy + y^2$.

2. $x^2 + 6xy + 9y^2$.

3. $x^2 + 16x + 64$.

4. $x^2 + 10ax + 25a^2$.

5. $a^2 - 16a + 64$.

6. $a^2 - 10ab + 25b^2$.

7. $c^2 - 6cd + 9d^2$.

8. $4x^2 - 4x + 1$.

9. $4a^2 - 12ab + 9b^2$.

10. $9a^2 - 24ab + 16b^2$.

11. $x^2 + 8xy + 16y^2$.

12. $x^2 - 8xy + 16y^2$.

13. $4x^2 - 20xy + 25y^2$.

14. $1 + 20a + 100a^2$.

15. $49a^2 - 28a + 4$.

16. $36a^2 + 60ab + 25b^2$.

17. $81x^2 - 36bx + 4b^2$.

18. $m^2n^2 + 14mnx^2 + 49x^2$.

Case VII.

115. When a trinomial has the form $x^2 + ax + b$.

Where a is the *algebraic sum* of two numbers, and is either positive or negative; and b is the *product* of these two numbers, and is either positive or negative.

Since $(x + 5)(x + 3) = x^2 + 8x + 15,$

the factors of $x^2 + 8x + 15$ are $x + 5$ and $x + 3$.

Since $(x + 5)(x - 3) = x^2 + 2x - 15,$

the factors of $x^2 + 2x - 15$ are $(x + 5)$ and $(x - 3)$.

Hence, if a trinomial of the form $x^2 + ax + b$ is such an expression that it can be resolved into two binomial factors, it is obvious that the first term of each factor will be x, and that the second terms of the factors will be two numbers whose product is b, the last term of the trinomial, and whose algebraic sum is a, the coefficient of x in the middle term of the trinomial.

1. Resolve into factors $x^2 + 11x + 30$.

We are required to find two numbers whose product is 30 and whose sum is 11.

Two numbers whose product is 30 are 1 and 30, 2 and 15, 3 and 10, 5 and 6, and the sum of the last two numbers is 11. Hence,

$$x^2 + 11x + 30 = (x + 5)(x + 6).$$

2. Resolve into factors $x^2 - 7x + 12$.

We are required to find two numbers whose product is 12 and whose algebraic sum is -7.

Since the product is $+12$, the two numbers are *both positive* or *both negative*, and since their sum is -7, they must both be negative.

Two negative numbers whose product is 12 are -12 and -1, -6 and -2, -4 and -3, and the sum of the last two numbers is -7. Hence,

$$x^2 - 7x + 12 = (x - 4)(x - 3).$$

3. Resolve into factors $x^2 + 2x - 24$.

We are required to find two numbers whose product is -24 and whose algebraic sum is 2.

Since the product is -24, one of the numbers is positive and the other negative, and since their sum is $+2$, the larger number is positive.

Two numbers whose product is -24, and the larger number positive, are 24 and -1, 12 and -2, 8 and -3, 6 and -4, and the sum of the last two numbers is $+2$. Hence,

$$x^2 + 2x - 24 = (x + 6)(x - 4).$$

4. Resolve into factors $x^2 - 3x - 18$.

Since the product is -18, one of the numbers is positive and the other negative, and since their sum is -3, the larger number is negative.

Two numbers whose product is -18, and the larger number negative, are -18 and 1, -9 and 2, -6 and 3, and the sum of the last two numbers is -3. Hence,

$$x^2 - 3x - 18 = (x - 6)(x + 3).$$

Exercise 38.

Resolve into factors:

1. $a^2 + 5a + 6.$

2. $a^2 - 5a + 6.$

3. $a^2 + 6a + 5.$

4. $a^2 - 6a + 5.$

5. $a^2 + 4a - 5.$

6. $a^2 - 4a - 5.$

7. $c^2 - 9c + 18.$

8. $c^2 + 9c + 18.$

9. $c^2 + 3c - 18.$

10. $c^2 - 3c - 18.$

11. $x^2 + 9x + 14.$

12. $x^2 - 9x + 14.$

13. $x^2 - 5x - 14.$

14. $x^2 - 9x + 20.$

15. $x^2 - x - 20.$

16. $x^2 + x - 20.$

17. $x^2 - 10x + 21.$

18. $x^2 - 4x - 21.$

19. $x^2 + 4x - 21.$

20. $x^2 - 15x + 56.$

21. $x^2 - x - 56.$

22. $x^2 - 10x + 9.$

23. $x^2 + 13x + 30.$

24. $x^2 + 7x - 30.$

25. $x^2 - 7x - 30.$

26. $a^2 + ab - 6b^2.$

27. $a^2 - ab - 6b^2.$

28. $a^2 + 3ab - 4b^2.$

29. $a^2 - 3ab - 4b^2.$

30. $a^2x^2 - 2ax - 63.$

31. $a^2 + 2ax - 63x^2.$

32. $a^2 - 9ab + 20b^2.$

33. $x^2y^2 - 19xyz + 48z^2.$

34. $a^2b^2 + 15abc + 44c^2$.

35. $x^2 - 13xy + 36y^2$.

36. $x^2 + 19xy + 84y^2$.

37. $a^2x^2 - 23axy + 102y^2$.

38. $x^4 - 9x^2y^2 + 20y^4$.

39. $a^4x^4 - 24a^2x^2y^2 + 143y^4$.

40. $a^6b^6 - 23a^3b^3c^2 + 132c^4$.

41. $a^2 - 20abc - 96b^2c^2$.

42. $a^2 - 4abc - 96b^2c^2$.

43. $a^2 - 10abc - 96b^2c^2$.

44. $a^2 + 29abc - 96b^2c^2$.

45. $a^2 - 46abc - 96b^2c^2$.

46. $a^2 + 49abc + 48b^2c^2$.

47. $x^2 - 18xyz - 243y^2z^2$.

48. $x^2y^2 - xyz - 182z^2$.

Exercise 39.

Examples For Review.

Resolve into factors:

1. $a^3 - 7a$.

2. $3a^2b^2 - 2a^3b + 3ab^3$.

3. $(a - b)^2 + (a - b)$.

4. $(a + b)^2 - 1$.

5. $a^3 + 8b^3$.

6. $(x^2 - 4y^2) + (x - 2y)$.

7. $(a^3 - b^3) + (a - b)$.

8. $a^2 - 6ab + 9b^2$.

9. $x^2 - x - 2$.

10. $x^2 - 2x - 3$.

11. $x^2 + 4x - 21$.

12. $a^2 - 11a - 26$.

13. $ax^2 + bx^2 + 3a + 3b.$

14. $x^2 - 3x - xy + 3y.$

15. $x^2 - 7x + 12.$

16. $a^2 + 5ab + 6b^2.$

17. $x^4 + 10x^2 + 25.$

18. $x^2 - 18x + 81.$

19. $x^2 - 21x + 110.$

20. $x^2 + 19x + 88.$

21. $x^2 - 19x + 88.$

22. $x^3 - x^2 + x - 1.$

23. $9x^4 - x^2.$

24. $1 - (a - b)^2.$

25. $(a^3 + b^3) + (a + b).$

26. $m^2x - n^2x + m^2y - n^2y.$

27. $(x - y)^2 - z^2.$

28. $z^2 - (x - y)^2.$

29. $4a^4 - (3a - 1)^2.$

30. $8x^3 - y^3.$

31. $x^3 - 3x^2y.$

32. $x^3 - 27y^3.$

33. $x^2 + 3x - 40.$

34. $x^2 + 3xy - 10y^2.$

35. $1 - 16x^2.$

36. $a^6 - 9a^2b^4.$

37. $x^3 + 3x^2y + 2xy^2.$

38. $x^4 + 4x^3y + 3x^2y^2.$

39. $x^2 - 4xy^2 + 4y^4.$

40. $16x^4 + 8x^2 + 1.$

41. $9a^4 - 4a^2c^2.$

42. $a^3b - a^2b^2 - 2ab^3.$

43. $x^4 - x^3 + 8x - 8.$

44. $a^4 - a^3x + ay^3 - xy^3.$

CHAPTER VIII.

COMMON FACTORS AND MULTIPLES.

116. Common Factors. A **common factor** of two or more *integral numbers* is an integral number which divides each of them without a remainder.

117. A **common factor** of two or more integral and rational *expressions* is an integral and rational expression which divides each of them without a remainder.

Thus $5a$ is a common factor of $20a$ and $25a$, $3x^2y^2$ is a common factor of $12x^2y^2$ and $15x^3y^3$.

118. Two *numbers* are said to be **prime** to each other when they have no common factor except 1.

119. Two *expressions* are said to be **prime** to each other when they have no common factor except 1.

120. The **highest common factor** of two or more integral *numbers* is the greatest number that will divide each of them without a remainder.

121. The **highest common factor** of two or more integral and rational *expressions* is an integral and rational expression of highest degree that will divide each of them without a remainder.

Thus $3a^2$ is the highest common factor of $3a^2$, $6a^3$, and $12a^4$, $5x^2y^2$ is the highest common factor of $10x^3y^2$ and $15x^2y^2$.

For brevity, we use H. C. F. for "highest common factor."

122. To Find the Highest Common Factor of Two or More Algebraic Expressions.

1. Find the H. C. F. of $42a^3b^2$ and $30a^2b^4$.

$$\begin{aligned} 42a^3b^2 &= 2 \times 3 \times 7 \times aaa \times bb; \\ 30a^2b^4 &= 2 \times 3 \times 5 \times aa \times bbbb. \\ \therefore \text{ the H. C. F.} &= 2 \times 3 \times aa \times bb, \quad \text{or} \quad 6a^2b^2. \end{aligned}$$

2. Find the H. C. F. of $x^2 - 9y^2$ and $x^2 + 6xy + 9y^2$.

$$\begin{aligned} x^2 - 9y^2 &= (x + 3y)(x - 3y); \\ x^2 + 6xy + 9y^2 &= (x + 3y)(x + 3y). \\ \therefore \text{ the H. C. F.} &= (x + 3y). \end{aligned}$$

3. Find the H. C. F. of $4x^2 - 4x - 80$, $2x^2 - 18x + 40$.

$$\begin{aligned} 4x^2 - 4x - 80 &= 4(x^2 - x - 20) \\ &= 4(x - 5)(x + 4); \\ 2x^2 - 18x + 40 &= 2(x^2 - 9x + 20) \\ &= 2(x - 5)(x - 4). \\ \therefore \text{ the H. C. F.} &= 2(x - 5). \end{aligned}$$

To find the H. C. F. of two or more expressions, therefore,

Resolve each expression into its simplest factors.

Find the product of all the common factors, taking each factor the least number of times it occurs in any of the given expressions.

NOTE. The *highest common factor* in Algebra corresponds to the *greatest common measure*, or *greatest common divisor* in Arithmetic. We cannot apply the terms *greatest* and *least* to an algebraic expression in which particular values have not been given to the letters contained in the expression. Thus a is *greater* than a^2, if a stands for $\frac{1}{4}$.

Exercise 40.

Find the H. C. F. of:

1. 330 and 546.

2. $20x^3$ and $15x^4$.

3. $42ax^2$ and $60a^2x$.

4. $35a^2b^2$ and $49ab^3$.

5. $28x^4$ and $63y^4$.

6. $54a^2b^2$ and $56a^3b^3$.

7. x^3+3x^2y and x^3+27y^3.

8. x^2+3x and x^2-9.

9. $2ax^3+x^3$ and $8a^3+1$.

10. $(x+y)^2$ and x^2-y^2.

11. a^3+a^2x and a^2-x^2.

12. a^2-4b^2 and a^2+2ab.

13. x^2-1 and x^2+2x-3.

14. x^2+5x+6 and x^2+4x+3.

15. $x^2-9x+18$ and $x^2-10x+24$.

16. $x^3 + 1$ and $x^2 - x + 1$.

17. $x^2 - 3x + 2$ and $x^2 - 4x + 3$.

18. $x^2 - 3xy + 2y^2$ and $x^2 - 2xy + y^2$.

19. $x^2 - 4x - 5$ and $x^2 - 25$.

20. $(a - b)^2 - c^2$ and $ab - b^2 - bc$.

21. $x^2 + xy - 2y^2$ and $x^2 + 5xy + 6y^2$.

22. $x^2 + 7xy + 12y^2$ and $x^2 + 3xy - 4y^2$.

23. $x^3 - 8y^3$ and $x^2 + 2xy + 4y^2$.

24. $x^3 - 2x^2 - x + 2$ and $x^2 - 4x + 4$.

25. $1 - 5a + 6a^2$ and $1 - 7a + 12a^2$.

26. $x^2 - 8xy + 7y^2$ and $x^2 - 3xy - 28y^2$.

27. $8a^3 + b^3$ and $4a^2 + 4ab + b^2$.

28. $x^2 - (y - z)^2$ and $(x + y)^2 - z^2$.

123. Common Multiples. A **common multiple** of two or more integral *numbers* is a number which is exactly divisible by each, of the numbers.

A **common multiple** of two or more *expressions* is an expression which is exactly divisible by each of the expressions.

124. The **lowest common multiple** of two or more *numbers* is the least number that is exactly divisible by each of the given numbers.

The **lowest common multiple** of two or more *expressions* is the expression of lowest degree that is exactly divisible by each of the given expressions.

We use L. C. M. for "lowest common multiple."

To find the lowest common multiple of two or more algebraic expressions.

1. Find the L. C. M. of $42a^3b^2$, $30a^2b^4$, and $66ab^3$.

$$\begin{aligned} 42a^3b^2 &= 2 \times 3 \times 7 \times a^3 \times b^2; \\ 30a^2b^4 &= 2 \times 3 \times 5 \times a^2 \times b^4; \\ 66ab^3 &= 2 \times 3 \times 11 \times a \times b^3. \end{aligned}$$

The L. C. M. must evidently contain each factor the greatest number of times that it occurs in any expression.

$$\begin{aligned} \therefore \text{ L. C. M.} &= 2 \times 3 \times 7 \times 5 \times 11a^3 \times b^4, \\ &= 2310a^3b^4. \end{aligned}$$

2. Find the L. C. M. of $4x^2 - 4x - 80$ and $2x^2 - 18x + 40$.

$$\begin{aligned} 4x^2 - 4x - 80 &= 4(x^2 - x - 20) = 4(x-5)(x+4); \\ 2x^2 - 18x + 40 &= 2(x^2 - 9x + 20) = 2(x-5)(x-4). \\ \therefore \text{ L. C. M.} &= 4(x-5)(x+4)(x-4). \end{aligned}$$

To find the L. C. M. of two or more expressions, therefore,

Resolve each expression into its simplest factors.

Find the product of all the different factors, taking each factor the greatest number of times it occurs in any of the given expressions.

Exercise 41.

Find the L. C. M. of:

1. $9xy^3$ and $6x^2y$.

2. $3abc^2$ and $2a^2bc^3$.

3. $4a^3b$ and $10ab^3$.

4. $6a^3b^3$ and $15a^2b^4$.

5. $21xy^3$ and $27x^3y^5$.

6. xy^3z^2 and $x^2y^2z^3$.

7. a^2 and $a^2 + a$.

8. x^2 and $x^3 - 3x^2$.

9. $x^2 - 1$ and $x^2 + x$.

10. $x^2 - 1$ and $x^2 - x$.

11. $x^2 + xy$ and $xy + y^2$.

12. $x^2 + 2x$ and $(x + 2)^2$.

13. $a^2 + 4a + 4$ and $a^2 + 5a + 6$.

14. $c^2 + c - 20$ and $c^2 - c - 30$.

15. $b^2 + b - 42$ and $b^2 - 11b + 30$.

16. $y^2 - 10y + 24$ and $y^2 + y - 20$.

17. $z^2 + 2z - 35$ and $z^2 - 11z + 30$.

18. $x^2 - 64; x^3 - 64$; and $x + 8$.

19. $a^2 - b^2; (a + b)^2$; and $(a - b)^2$.

20. $4ab(a + b)^2$ and $2a^2(a^2 - b^2)$.

21. $y^2 + 7y + 12; y^2 + 6y + 8$; and $y^2 + 5y + 6$.

22. $x^2 - 1; x^3 + x^2 + x + 1$; and $x^3 - x^2 + x - 1$.

23. $1 - x^2; 1 - x^3$; and $1 + x$.

24. $x^2 + 2xy + y^2; x^2 - y^2$; and $x^2 - 2xy + y^2$.

25. $x^3 - 27; x^2 + 2x - 15; x^2 + 5x$.

26. $(a + b)^2 - c^2; (a + b + c)^2$; and $a + b - c$.

27. $x^2 - (a + b)x + ab$ and $x^2 - (a + c)x + ac$.

28. $(a + b)^2 - c^2$ and $a^2 + ab + ac$.

CHAPTER IX.

FRACTIONS.

125. An **algebraic fraction** is the indicated quotient of two expressions, written in the form $dfracab$.

The dividend a is called the **numerator**, and the divisor b is called the **denominator**; and the numerator and denominator are called the **terms** of the fraction.

126. The introduction of the same factor into the dividend and divisor does not alter the value of the quotient, and the rejection of the same factor from the dividend and divisor does not alter the value of the quotient.

Thus $\frac{12}{4} = 3; \quad \frac{2 \times 12}{2 \times 4} = 3; \frac{12 \div 2}{4 \div 2} = 3.$ Hence,

The value of a fraction is not altered if the numerator and denominator are both multiplied, or both divided, by the same factor.

Reduction of Fractions.

127. To reduce a fraction is to change its *form* without altering its *value.*

CASE I.

128. To Reduce a Fraction to its Lowest Terms.

A fraction is in its *lowest terms* when the numerator and denominator have no common factor. We have, therefore, the following rule:

Resolve the numerator and denominator into their prime factors, and cancel all the common factors.

Reduce the following fractions to their lowest terms:

1. $\dfrac{38a^2b^3c^4}{57a^3bc^2} = \dfrac{2\times 19a^2b^3c^4}{3\times 19a^3bc^2} = \dfrac{2b^2c^2}{3a}.$

2. $\dfrac{a^3-x^3}{a^2-x^2} = \dfrac{(a-x)(a^2+ax+x^2)}{(a-x)(a+x)} = \dfrac{a^2+ax+x^2}{a+x}.$

3. $\dfrac{a^2+7a+10}{a^2+5a+6} = \dfrac{(a+5)(a+2)}{(a+3)(a+2)} = \dfrac{a+5}{a+3}.$

Exercise 42.

Reduce to lowest terms:

1. $\dfrac{2a}{6ab}.$
2. $\dfrac{12m^2n}{15mn^2}.$
3. $\dfrac{21m^2p^2}{28mp^4}.$
4. $\dfrac{3x^3y^2z}{6xy^3z^2}.$
5. $\dfrac{5a^3b^3c^3}{15c^5}.$
6. $\dfrac{34x^3y^4z^5}{51x^2y^3z^5}.$
7. $\dfrac{46m^2np^3}{69mnp^4}.$
8. $\dfrac{39a^2b^3c^4}{52a^5bc^3}.$
9. $\dfrac{58xy^4z^6}{87xy^2z^2}.$

10. $\dfrac{abx - bx^2}{acx - cx^2}$.

11. $\dfrac{4a^2 - 9b^2}{4a^2 + 6ab}$.

12. $\dfrac{3a^2 + 6a}{a^2 + 4a + 4}$.

13. $\dfrac{x^2 + 5x}{x^2 + 4x - 5}$.

14. $\dfrac{xy - 3y^2}{x^3 - 27y^3}$.

15. $\dfrac{x^2 + 5x + 4}{x^2 - x - 20}$.

16. $\dfrac{x^2 + 2x + 1}{x^2 - x - 2}$.

17. $\dfrac{(a + b)^2 - c^2}{a^2 + ab - ac}$.

18. $\dfrac{x^2 + 9x + 20}{x^2 + 7x + 12}$.

19. $\dfrac{x^2 - 14x - 15}{x^2 - 12x - 45}$.

Case II.

129. To Reduce a Fraction to an Integral or Mixed Expression.

1. Reduce $\dfrac{x^3 - 1}{x - 1}$ to an integral or mixed expression.

By division, $\dfrac{x^3 - 1}{x - 1} = x^2 + x + 1.$

2. Reduce $\dfrac{x^3 - 1}{x + 1}$ to an integral or mixed expression.

By division, $\dfrac{x^3 - 1}{x + 1} = x^2 - x + 1 - \dfrac{2}{x + 1}.$

To reduce a fraction to an integral or mixed expression, therefore,

Divide the numerator by the denominator.

NOTE. If there is a remainder, this remainder must be written as the numerator of a fraction of which the divisor is the denominator, and this fraction with its proper sign must be annexed to the integral part of the quotient.

Exercise 43.

Reduce to integral or mixed expressions:

1. $\dfrac{a^2-b^2+2}{a-b}$.

2. $\dfrac{a^2-b^2-2}{a+b}$.

3. $\dfrac{a^3-2a^2+2a+1}{a^2-a-1}$.

4. $\dfrac{2x^2-2x+1}{x+1}$.

5. $\dfrac{8x^3}{2x+1}$.

6. $\dfrac{5x^3+9x^2+3}{x^2+x-1}$.

7. $\dfrac{a^3+a^2+7a-2}{a^2+a+2}$.

8. $\dfrac{y^4+y^2x^2+x^4}{y^2+yx+x^2}$.

9. $\dfrac{x^4-3x^3+x-1}{x^2+x+1}$.

10. $\dfrac{x^5-x^4+1}{x^2-x-1}$.

CASE III.

130. To Reduce a Mixed Expression to a Fraction.

The process is precisely the same as in Arithmetic. Hence,

Multiply the integral expression by the denominator, to the product add the numerator, and under the result write the denominator.

Reduce to a fraction $a - b - \dfrac{a^2 - ab - b^2}{a + b}$.

$$a - b - \frac{a^2 - ab - b^2}{a + b} = \frac{(a - b)(a + b) - (a^2 - ab - b^2)}{a + b}$$
$$= \frac{a^2 - b^2 - a^2 + ab + b^2}{a + b}$$
$$= \frac{ab}{a + b}.$$

NOTE. The dividing line between the terms of a fraction has the force of a vinculum affecting the numerator. If, therefore, a *minus sign* precedes the dividing line, as in the preceding Example, and this line is removed, the numerator of the given fraction must be enclosed in a parenthesis preceded by the minus sign, or the sign of every term of the numerator must be changed.

Exercise 44.

Reduce to a fraction:

1. $x - y + \dfrac{2xy}{x - y}$.

2. $x + y - \dfrac{2xy}{x + y}$.

3. $1 - \dfrac{x - y}{x + y}$.

4. $a - x - \dfrac{a^2 + x^2}{a - x}$.

5. $x + 2 - \dfrac{x^2 - 4}{x - 3}$.

6. $\dfrac{x - 3}{x - 2} - 2x + 1$.

7. $\dfrac{x + 3}{x + 2} + x^2 - x - 1$.

8. $2a - 1 + \dfrac{3 - 4a}{a - 3}$.

9. $1 - 2a^2 - \dfrac{a^2 - a + 2}{a - 1}$.

10. $a^2 + 2a - 5 - \dfrac{2a - 1}{3a^2 + 1}$.

Case IV.

131. To Reduce Fractions to their Lowest Common Denominator.

The process is the same as in Arithmetic. Hence:

Find the lowest common multiple of the denominators; this will be the required denominator. Divide this denominator by the denominator of each fraction.

Multiply the first numerator by the first quotient, the second numerator by the second quotient, and so on.

The products will be the respective numerators of the equivalent fractions.

NOTE. Every fraction should be in its lowest terms before the common denominator is found.

1. Reduce $\frac{3x}{4a^2}$, $\frac{2y}{3a}$, and $\frac{5}{6a^3}$ to equivalent fractions having the lowest common denominator.

The L. C. M. of $4a^2$, $3a$, and $6a^3 = 12a^3$.

The respective quotients are $3a$, $4a^2$, and 2.

The products are $9ax$, $8a^2y$, and 10.

Hence, the required fractions are

$$\frac{9ax}{12a^3}, \quad \frac{8a^2y}{12a^3}, \quad \text{and} \quad \frac{10}{12a^3}.$$

2. Express $\frac{1}{x^2+5x+6}$ and $\frac{1}{x^2+4x+3}$ with lowest common denominator.

The factors of the denominators are $x+3$, $x+2$; and $x+3$, $x+1$.

Hence the lowest common denominator (L. C. D.) is $(x+3)(x+2)(x+1)$, and the required numerators are $x+1$ and $x+2$. Hence the required fractions are

$$\frac{x+1}{(x+3)(x+2)(x+1)} \quad \text{and} \quad \frac{x+2}{(x+3)(x+2)(x+1)}.$$

Exercise 45.

Express with lowest common denominator:

1. $\dfrac{x}{x-a}, \dfrac{x^2}{x^2-a^2}.$

2. $\dfrac{a}{a+b}, \dfrac{a^2}{a^2-b^2}.$

3. $\dfrac{1}{1+2a}, \dfrac{1}{1-4a^2}.$

4. $\dfrac{9}{16-x^2}, \dfrac{4-x}{4+x}.$

5. $\dfrac{a^2}{27-a^3}, \dfrac{a}{3-a}.$

6. $\dfrac{1}{x^2-5x+6}, \dfrac{1}{x^2-x-6}.$

Addition and Subtraction of Fractions.

132. The algebraic sum of two or more fractions which have the same denominator, is a fraction whose numerator is the algebraic sum of the numerators of the given fractions, and whose denominator is the common denominator of the given fractions. Hence,

To add fractions,

Reduce the fractions to equivalent fractions having the same denominator; and write the algebraic sum of the numerators of these fractions over the common denominator.

133. When the denominators are simple expressions.

1. Simplify $\dfrac{3a-4b}{4} - \dfrac{2a-b+c}{3} + \dfrac{a-4c}{12}.$

The L. C. D. = 12.

The multipliers, that is, the quotients obtained by dividing 12 by 4, 3, and 12, are 3, 4, and 1.

Hence the sum of the fractions equals

$$\frac{9a-12b}{12}-\frac{8a-4b+4c}{12}+\frac{a-4c}{12}$$
$$=\frac{9a-12b-8a+4b-4c+a-4c}{12}$$
$$=\frac{2a-8b-8c}{12}=\frac{a-4b-4c}{6}.$$

The preceding work may be arranged as follows:

The L. C. D. = 12.

The multipliers are 3, 4, and 1, respectively.

$$\begin{array}{rcll} 3(3a - 4b \quad\quad) &=& 9a - 12b & = \text{1st numerator.}\\ -4(2a - b + c) &=& -8a + 4b - 4c & = \text{2d numerator.}\\ 1(a - \quad 4c) &=& \underline{a \quad\quad\quad - 4c} & = \text{3d numerator.}\\ && 2a - 8b - 8c & \\ && \text{or } 2(a - 4b - 4c) & = \text{the sum of the numerators.} \end{array}$$

$$\therefore \text{ sum of fractions} = \frac{2(a-4b-4c)}{12}=\frac{a-4b-4c}{6}.$$

Exercise 46.

Find the sum of:

1. $\dfrac{x+1}{2}+\dfrac{x-3}{5}+\dfrac{x+5}{10}.$

2. $\dfrac{2x-1}{3}+\dfrac{x+5}{4}+\dfrac{x-4}{6}.$

3. $\dfrac{7x-1}{6}-\dfrac{3x-2}{7}+\dfrac{x-5}{3}.$

4. $\dfrac{3x-2}{9}-\dfrac{x-2}{6}+\dfrac{5x+3}{4}.$

5. $\dfrac{x-1}{6}-\dfrac{x-3}{3}+\dfrac{x-5}{2}.$

6. $\dfrac{x-2y}{2x}+\dfrac{x+5y}{4x}-\dfrac{x+7y}{8x}.$

7. $\dfrac{5x-11}{3}-\dfrac{2x-1}{10}-\dfrac{11x-5}{15}.$

8. $\dfrac{x-3}{3x}-\dfrac{x^2-6x}{5x^2}-\dfrac{7x^2-x^3}{15x^3}.$

9. $\dfrac{ac-b^2}{ac}-\dfrac{ab-c^2}{ab}+\dfrac{a^2-bc}{bc}.$

134. When the denominators have compound expressions, arranged in the same order.

1. Simplify $\dfrac{a+b}{a-b}-\dfrac{a-b}{a+b}-\dfrac{4ab}{a^2-b^2}.$

The L. C. D. is $(a-b)(a+b)$.

The multipliers are $a+b$, $a-b$, and 1, respectively.

$$\begin{array}{lcll}
(a+b)(a+b) &=& a^2+2ab+b^2 &= \text{1st numerator.}\\
-(a-b)(a-b) &=& -a^2+2ab-b^2 &= \text{2d numerator.}\\
-1(4ab) &=& \underline{\quad -4ab \quad} &= \text{3d numerator.}\\
 & & 0 &= \text{sum of numerators.}
\end{array}$$

$\therefore$ Sum of fractions $= 0$.

Exercise 47.

Find the sum of:

1. $\frac{1}{x+3}+\frac{1}{x-2}.$

2. $\frac{1}{x+1}+\frac{1}{x-1}.$

3. $\frac{4}{x-8}-\frac{1}{x+2}.$

4. $\frac{a+x}{a-x}-\frac{a-x}{a+x}.$

5. $\frac{x}{x-a}-\frac{x^2}{x^2-a^2}.$

6. $\frac{4a^2+b^2}{4a^2-b^2}-\frac{2a+b}{2a-b}.$

7. $\frac{7}{9-a^2}-\frac{1}{3+a}-\frac{1}{3-a}.$

8. $\frac{1}{a-b}-\frac{1}{a+b}-\frac{b}{a^2-b^2}.$

9. $\frac{2}{x-2}-\frac{2}{x+2}+\frac{5x}{x^2-4}.$

10. $\frac{3-x}{1-3x}-\frac{3+x}{1+3x}-\frac{15x-1}{1-9x^2}.$

11. $\frac{1}{a}-\frac{1}{a+3}+\frac{3}{a+1}.$

12. $\frac{x}{x-1}-\frac{1}{-}\frac{1}{x+1}.$

13. $\frac{x+1}{x+2}+\frac{x-2}{x-3}+\frac{2x+7}{x^2-x-6}.$

14. $\frac{1}{x(x-1)}-\frac{2}{x^2-1}+\frac{1}{x(x+1)}.$

Exercise 48.

Find the sum of:

1. $\dfrac{1}{2x+1}+\dfrac{1}{2x-1}-\dfrac{4x}{4x^2-1}.$

2. $\dfrac{a^2+b^2}{a^2-b^2}+\dfrac{a}{a+b}-\dfrac{b}{a-b}.$

3. $\dfrac{3a}{1-a^2}+\dfrac{2}{1-a}-\dfrac{2}{1+a}.$

4. $\dfrac{1}{2x+5y}-\dfrac{3x}{4x^2-25y^2}+\dfrac{1}{2x+5y}.$

5. $\dfrac{1}{x+4y}-\dfrac{8y}{x^2-16y^2}+\dfrac{1}{x-4y}.$

6. $\dfrac{3}{2x-3}-\dfrac{2}{2x+3}-\dfrac{3}{4x^2-9}.$

Multiplication and Division of Fractions.

135. Find the product of $\frac{a}{b} \times \frac{c}{d}$.

Let $\frac{a}{b} = x$, and $\frac{c}{d} = y$.

Then $a = bx$, and $c = dy$.

The product of these two equations is

$$ac = bdxy.$$

Divide by bd, $\qquad \frac{ac}{bd} = xy.$

But $\qquad \frac{a}{b} \times \frac{c}{d} = xy.$

Therefore $\qquad \frac{a}{b} \times \frac{c}{d} = \frac{ac}{bd}.$

To find the product of two fractions, therefore,

Find the product of the numerators for the required numerator, and the product of the denominators for the required denominator.

In like manner,

$$\frac{a}{b} \times \frac{c}{d} \times \frac{e}{f} = \frac{ac}{bd} \times \frac{e}{f} = \frac{ace}{bdf}.$$

136. Reciprocals. If the product of two numbers is equal to 1, each of the numbers is called the **reciprocal** of the other.

The reciprocal of $\frac{a}{b}$ is $\frac{b}{a}$, for $\frac{b}{a} \times \frac{a}{b} = \frac{ba}{ab} = 1.$

The reciprocal of a fraction, therefore, is the fraction inverted.

Since $\frac{a}{b} \div \frac{a}{b} = 1$, and $\frac{b}{a} \times \frac{a}{b} = 1$, it follows that

To divide by a fraction is the same as to multiply by its reciprocal.

137. To Divide by a Fraction, therefore,

Invert the divisor and multiply.

NOTE. Every mixed expression should first be reduced to a fraction, and every integral expression should be written as a fraction having 1 for the denominator. Both terms of each fraction should be expressed in their prime factors, and if a factor is common to a numerator and denominator, it should be cancelled, as the cancelling of a common factor *before* the multiplication is evidently equivalent to cancelling it *after* the multiplication.

1. Find the product of $\frac{3a^2b}{2x^2y} \times \frac{6xy^2}{7ab} \times \frac{7abc}{9a^2by^2}$.

$$\frac{3a^2b}{2x^2y} \times \frac{6xy^2}{7ab} \times \frac{7abc}{9a^2by^2} = \frac{3 \times 6 \times 7a^3b^2cxy^2}{2 \times 7 \times 9a^3b^2x^2y^3} = \frac{c}{xy}.$$

2. Find the product of $\frac{ab - b^2}{a + b} \times \frac{ab + b^2}{a^2 - b^2}$.

$$\frac{ab - b^2}{a + b} \times \frac{ab + b^2}{a^2 - b^2} = \frac{b(a - b)}{(a + b)} \times \frac{b(a + b)}{(a - b)(a + b)} = \frac{b^2}{a + b}.$$

3. Find quotient of $\dfrac{ab}{(a-b)^2} \div \dfrac{ac}{a^2-b^2}$.

$$\begin{aligned}\frac{ab}{(a-b)^2} \div \frac{ac}{a^2-b^2} &= \frac{ab}{(a-b)(a-b)} \times \frac{(a-b)(a+b)}{ac} \\ &= \frac{b(a+b)}{c(a-b)}.\end{aligned}$$

4. Find the result of $\dfrac{1}{x} \times \dfrac{x^2-1}{x^2-4x-5} \div \dfrac{x^2+2x-3}{x^2-25}$.

$$\begin{aligned}&\frac{1}{x} \times \frac{x^2-1}{x^2-4x-5} \div \frac{x^2+2x-3}{x^2-25} \\ &\quad= \frac{1}{x} \times \frac{x^2-1}{x^2-4x-5} \times \frac{x^2-25}{x^2+2x-3} \\ &\quad= \frac{1}{x} \times \frac{(x-1)(x+1)}{(x-5)(x+1)} \times \frac{(x-5)(x+5)}{(x+3)(x-1)} \\ &\quad= \frac{x+5}{x(x+3)}.\end{aligned}$$

Exercise 49.

Express in the simplest form:

1. $\dfrac{15a^2}{7b^2} \times \dfrac{28ab}{9a^3c}$.

2. $\dfrac{3x^2y^2z^3}{4a^2b^2c^2} \times \dfrac{8a^3b^2c^2}{9x^2yz^3}$.

3. $\dfrac{5m^2n^2p^4}{3x^2yz^3} \times \dfrac{21xyz^2}{20m^2n^2p^2}$.

4. $\dfrac{16a^4b^2c^3}{21m^2x^3y^4} \times \dfrac{3m^3x^3y^4}{8a^2b^2c^2}$.

5. $\frac{2a}{bc} \times \frac{3b}{ac} \times \frac{5c}{ab}$.

6. $\frac{2a^3}{3bc} \times \frac{3b^3}{5ac} \times \frac{5c^3}{2ab}$.

7. $\frac{5abc^3}{3x^2} \div \frac{10ac^3}{6bx^2}$.

8. $\frac{x^2 - a^2}{x^2 - 4a^2} \times \frac{x + 2a}{x - a}$.

9. $\frac{x^2y^2 + 3xy}{4c^2 - 1} \times \frac{2c + 1}{xy + 3}$.

10. $\frac{a^2 - 100}{a^2 - 9} \times \frac{a - 3}{a - 10}$.

11. $\frac{9x^2 - 4y^2}{x^2 - 4} \times \frac{x + 2}{3x - 2y}$.

12. $\frac{25a^2 - b^2}{16a^2 - 9b^2} \div \frac{5a - b}{4a - 3b}$.

13. $\frac{x^2 - 49}{(a + b)^2 - c^2} \div \frac{x + 7}{(a + b) - c}$.

14. $\frac{x^2 + 2x + 1}{x^2 - 25} \div \frac{x + 1}{x^2 + 5x}$.

15. $\frac{a^2 + 3a + 2}{a^2 + 5a + 6} \times \frac{a^2 + 7a + 12}{a^2 + 9a + 20}$.

16. $\frac{y^2 - y - 30}{y^2 - 36} \times \frac{y^2 - y - 2}{y^2 + 3y - 10} \times \frac{y^2 + 6y}{y^2 + y}$.

17. $\frac{x^2 - 2x + 1}{x^2 - y^2} \times \frac{x^2 + 2xy + y^2}{x - 1} \div \frac{x^2 - 1}{x^2 - xy}$.

18. $\frac{a^2 - b^2}{a^2 - 3ab + 2b^2} \times \frac{ab - 2b^2}{a^2 + ab} \div \frac{(a - b)^2}{a(a - b)}$.

19. $\frac{(a + b)^2 - c^2}{a^2 + ab - ac} \times \frac{a^2b^2c^2}{a^2 + ab + ac} \div \frac{b^2c^2}{abc}$.

20. $\dfrac{x^2+7xy+10y^2}{x^2+6xy+5y^2} \times \dfrac{x+1}{x^2+4x+4} \div \dfrac{1}{x+2}.$

138. Complex Fractions. A complex fraction is one that has a fraction in the numerator, or in the denominator, or in both.

The shortest way to reduce to its simplest form a complex fraction is to multiply both terms of the fraction by the L. C. D. of the fractions contained in the numerator and denominator.

1. Simplify $\dfrac{3x}{x-\frac{1}{4}}.$

Multiply both terms by 4, and we have

$$\frac{12x}{4x-1}.$$

2. Simplify $\dfrac{\dfrac{a+x}{a-x}-\dfrac{a-x}{a+x}}{\dfrac{a+x}{a-x}+\dfrac{a-x}{a+x}}.$

The L. C. D. of the fractions in the numerator and denominator is

$$(a-x)(a+x).$$

Multiply by $(a-x)(a+x)$, and the result is

$$\begin{aligned}&\frac{(a+x)^2-(a-x)^2}{(a+x)^2+(a-x)^2}\\&\qquad=\frac{(a^2+2ax+x^2)-(a^2-2ax+x^2)}{(a^2+2ax+x^2)+(a^2-2ax+x^2)}\\&\qquad=\frac{a^2+2ax+x^2-a^2+2ax-x^2}{a^2+2ax+x^2+a^2-2ax+x^2}\\&\qquad=\frac{4ax}{2a^2+2x^2}\\&\qquad=\frac{2ax}{a^2+x^2}.\end{aligned}$$

Exercise 50.

Reduce to the simplest form:

1. $\dfrac{\dfrac{x}{b}+\dfrac{y}{b}}{\dfrac{z}{b}}$.

2. $\dfrac{x+\dfrac{y}{4}}{x-\dfrac{y}{3}}$.

3. $\dfrac{\dfrac{ab}{7}-3d}{3c-\dfrac{ab}{d}}$.

4. $\dfrac{1+\dfrac{1}{x+1}}{1-\dfrac{1}{x-1}}$.

5. $\dfrac{\dfrac{2m+x}{m+x}-1}{1-\dfrac{x}{m+x}}$.

6. $\dfrac{\dfrac{x+y}{x^2-y^2}}{\dfrac{x-y}{x+y}}$.

7. $\dfrac{a+\dfrac{ab}{a-b}}{a-\dfrac{ab}{a+b}}$.

8. $\dfrac{9a^2-64}{a-1-\dfrac{a+4}{4}}$.

9. $\dfrac{\dfrac{1}{x}+\dfrac{1}{y}}{\dfrac{1}{x}-\dfrac{1}{y}}$.

10. $\dfrac{x+3+\dfrac{2}{x}}{1+\dfrac{3}{x}+\dfrac{2}{x^2}}$.

11. $\dfrac{\dfrac{1}{x}-\dfrac{2}{x^2}+\dfrac{1}{x^3}}{\dfrac{(1-x)^2}{x^2}}$.

12. $\dfrac{x^2-x-6}{1-\dfrac{4}{x^2}}$.

13. $\dfrac{a^2-a+\dfrac{a-1}{a+1}}{a+\dfrac{1}{a+1}}$.

14. $\dfrac{\dfrac{4a(a-x)}{a^2-x^2}}{\dfrac{a-x}{a+x}}$.

CHAPTER X.

FRACTIONAL EQUATIONS.

139. To Reduce Equations containing Fractions.

1. Solve $\frac{x}{3} - \frac{x-1}{11} = x - 9.$

Multiply by 33, the L. C. M. of the denominators.

Then, $\quad 11x - 3x + 3 = 33x - 297.$

Transpose, $\quad 11x - 3x - 33x = -297 - 3.$

Combine, $\quad -25x = -300.$

Divide by -25, $\quad x = 12.$

NOTE. Since the minus sign precedes the second fraction, in removing the denominator, the $+$ (understood) before x, the first term of the numerator, is changed to $-$, and the $-$ before 1, the second term of the numerator, is changed to $+$.

To clear an equation of fractions, therefore,

Multiply each term by the L. C. M. of the denominators.

If a fraction is preceded by a **minus sign**, *the sign of every term of the numerator must be changed when the denominator is removed.*

2. Solve $\frac{x+1}{4} - \frac{1}{5}(x-1) = 1.$

Multiply by 20, the L. C. D.

$$5x + 5 - 4(x - 1) = 20.$$

$$5x + 5 - 4x + 4 = 20.$$

Transpose, $5x - 4x = 20 - 5 - 4.$

Combine, $x = 11.$

3. Solve

$$7x - \frac{(2x-3)(3x-5)}{5} = \frac{153}{10} - \frac{(4x-5)(3x-1)}{10}.$$

Multiply by 10, the L. C. D., and we have

$$70x - 2(2x-3)(3x-5) = 153 - (4x-5)(3x-1).$$

Find the products of $(2x - 3)(3x - 5)$ and $(4x - 5)(3x - 1)$.

$$70x - 2(6x^2 - 19x + 15) = 153 - (12x^2 - 19x + 5).$$

Remove the parentheses,

$$70x - 12x^2 + 38x - 30 = 153 - 12x^2 + 19x - 5.$$

Cancel the $-12x^2$ on each side and transpose,

$$70x + 38x - 19x = 153 + 30 - 5.$$

Combine, $89x = 178.$

Divide by 89, $x = 2.$

4. Solve $\dfrac{2x+1}{2x-1} - \dfrac{2x-1}{2x+1} = \dfrac{8}{4x^2-1}.$

Since $\qquad 4x^2 - 1 = (2x+1)(2x-1),$

the L. C. D. $\qquad = (2x+1)(2x-1).$

Multiply by the L. C. D., and we have,

$$4x^2 + 4x + 1 - (4x^2 - 4x + 1) = 8.$$
$$\therefore 4x^2 + 4x + 1 - 4x^2 + 4x - 1 = 8.$$
$$\therefore 8x = 8.$$
$$\therefore x = 1.$$

5. Solve $\dfrac{4}{x+1} - \dfrac{x+1}{x-1} + \dfrac{x^2-3}{x^2-1} = 0.$

Since $\qquad x^2 - 1 = (x+1)(x-1)$

the L. C. D. $\qquad = (x+1)(x-1).$

Multiply by the L. C. D., $x^2 - 1$, and we have,

$$4(x-1) - (x+1)(x+1) + x^2 - 3 = 0.$$
$$\therefore 4x - 4 - x^2 - 2x - 1 + x^2 - 3 = 0.$$
$$\therefore 2x = 8.$$
$$\therefore x = 4.$$

Exercise 51.

Solve:

1. $\frac{x-1}{2}=\frac{x+1}{3}.$

3. $\frac{6x-19}{2}=\frac{2x-11}{3}.$

2. $\frac{3x-1}{4}=\frac{2x+1}{3}.$

4. $\frac{7x-40}{8}=\frac{9x-80}{10}.$

5. $\frac{3x-116}{4}+\frac{180-5x}{6}=0.$

6. $\frac{3x-4}{2}-\frac{3x-1}{16}=\frac{6x-5}{8}.$

7. $\frac{x-1}{8}-\frac{x+1}{18}=1.$

8. $\frac{60-x}{14}-\frac{3x-5}{7}=\frac{3x}{4}.$

9. $\frac{3x-1}{11}-\frac{2-x}{10}=\frac{6}{5}.$

10. $\frac{4x}{x+1}-\frac{x}{x-2}=3.$

11. $\frac{2x+1}{4}-\frac{4x-1}{10}+1-\frac{1}{4}=0.$

12. $\frac{x-1}{5}-\frac{43-5x}{6}-\frac{3x-1}{8}=0.$

13. $\frac{1}{x+7}=\frac{2}{x+1}-\frac{1}{x+3}.$

14. $\dfrac{1}{x+4}+\dfrac{2}{x+6}-\dfrac{3}{x+5}=0.$

15. $\dfrac{4}{x^2-1}+\dfrac{1}{x-1}+\dfrac{1}{x+1}=0.$

16. $\dfrac{3x+1}{4}-\dfrac{5x-4}{7}=12-2x-\dfrac{x-2}{3}.$

17. $\frac{1}{8}(5x+3)-\frac{1}{3}(3-4x)+\frac{1}{6}(9-5x)=\frac{1}{2}(31-x).$

18. $\frac{1}{15}(34x-56)-\frac{1}{5}(7x-3)-\frac{1}{3}(7x-5)=0.$

Exercise 52.

Solve:

1. $\frac{2}{3}(x+1)-\frac{1}{7}(x+5)=1.$

2. $\frac{6}{7}(x-9)-\frac{1}{3}(5-x)+3x+1=0.$

3. $\frac{1}{3}(5x-24)+\frac{1}{7}(x-2)-2(x-1)=0.$

4. $\dfrac{x+3}{4}+\dfrac{7x-2}{5}=\dfrac{5x-1}{4}+\dfrac{5x+4}{9}.$

5. $\dfrac{x+1}{3}-\dfrac{x-1}{4}=\dfrac{x-2}{5}-\dfrac{x-3}{6}+\dfrac{31}{60}.$

6. $\dfrac{(2x-1)(2-x)}{2}+x^2-\dfrac{1+3x}{2}=0.$

7. $\dfrac{6x-11}{4}-\dfrac{3-4x}{6}=\dfrac{4}{3}-\dfrac{x}{8}.$

8. $\dfrac{x+6}{4} - \dfrac{16-3x}{12} = 4\tfrac{1}{6}.$

9. $x - \dfrac{x-2}{3} = \dfrac{x+23}{4} - \dfrac{10+x}{5}.$

10. $\dfrac{5x+3}{x-1} + \dfrac{2x-3}{2x-1} = 6.$

11. $\dfrac{3x}{4x+1} + 1 = 2 - \dfrac{x}{2(2x-1)}.$

12. $\dfrac{8x+7}{5x+4} - 1 = 1 - \dfrac{2x}{5x+1}.$

13. $\dfrac{x+1}{2(x-1)} - \dfrac{x-1}{x+1} = \dfrac{17-x^2}{2(x^2-1)}.$

140. If the denominators contain both simple and compound expressions, it is generally best to remove the simple expressions first, and then the compound expressions. After each multiplication the result should be reduced to the simplest form.

1. Solve $\dfrac{4x+3}{10} - \dfrac{2x+3}{5x-1} = \dfrac{2x-1}{5}.$

Multiply by 10, $\qquad 4x+3 - \dfrac{10(2x+3)}{5x-1} = 4x-2.$

Transpose, $\qquad 4x+3-4x+2 = \dfrac{10(2x+3)}{5x-1}.$

Combine, $\qquad 5 = \dfrac{10(2x+3)}{5x-1}.$

Divide by 5, $$1 = \frac{2(2x+3)}{5x-1}.$$

Multiply by $5x - 1$, $$5x - 1 = 4x + 6.$$

Transpose and combine, $$x = 7.$$

Exercise 53.

Solve:

1. $\dfrac{10x+13}{18} - \dfrac{x+2}{x-3} = \dfrac{5x-4}{9}.$

2. $\dfrac{6x+7}{10} - \dfrac{3x+1}{5} = \dfrac{x-1}{3x-4}.$

3. $\dfrac{11x-12}{14} - \dfrac{11x-7}{19x+7} = \dfrac{22x-36}{28}.$

4. $\dfrac{2x-1}{5} + \dfrac{2x-3}{17x-12} = \dfrac{4x-3}{10}.$

5. $\dfrac{11x-13}{7} - \dfrac{13x+7}{3x+7} = \dfrac{22x-75}{14}.$

6. $\dfrac{6x-13}{2x+3} + \dfrac{6x+7}{9} - \dfrac{2x+4}{3} = 0.$

141. Literal Equations. Literal equations are equations in which some or all of the known numbers are represented by letters; the numbers regarded as known numbers are usually represented by the *first* letters of the alphabet.

1. Solve $\dfrac{x+a}{x-b} + \dfrac{x+b}{x-a} = 2.$

Multiply by $(x-a)(x-b)$,

$$(x+a)(x-a)+(x+b)(x-b)=2(x-a)(x-b),$$

or

$$x^2-a^2+x^2-b^2=2x^2-2ax-2bx+2ab.$$

Transpose, $x^2+x^2-2x^2+2ax+2bx=a^2+2ab+b^2.$

Combine, $2ax+2bx=a^2+2ab+b^2,$

or

$$2(a+b)x=a^2+2ab+b^2.$$

Divide by $a+b$, $2x=a+b,$

$$\therefore x=\frac{a+b}{2}.$$

Exercise 54.

Solve:

1. $a(x-a)=b(x-b).$

2. $(a+b)x+(a-b)x=a^2.$

3. $(a+b)x-(a-b)x=b^2.$

4. $(2x-a)+(x-2a)=3a.$

5. $(x+a+b)+(x+a-b)=2b.$

6. $(x-a)(x-b)=x(x+c).$

7. $x^2+b^2=(a-x)(a-x).$

8. $(a+b)(2-x)=(a-b)(2+x).$

9. $(x-a)(2x-a)=2(x-b)^2.$

10. $(a + bx)(c + d) = (a + b)(c + dx)$.

11. $\dfrac{x}{a-b} - \dfrac{3a}{a+b} = \dfrac{bx}{a^2-b^2}$.

142. Problems involving Fractional Equations.

Exercise 55.

Ex. The sum of the third and fifth parts of a certain number exceeds two times the difference of the fourth and sixth parts by 22. Find the number.

Let $x =$ the number.

Then $\dfrac{x}{3} + \dfrac{x}{5} =$ the sum of its third and fifth parts,

$\dfrac{x}{4} - \dfrac{x}{6} =$ the difference of its fourth and sixth parts,

$2\left(\dfrac{x}{4} - \dfrac{x}{6}\right) =$ 2 times the difference of its fourth and sixth parts,

$\dfrac{x}{3} + \dfrac{x}{5} - 2\left(\dfrac{x}{4} - \dfrac{x}{6}\right) =$ the given excess.

But $22 =$ the given excess.

$$\therefore \frac{x}{3} + \frac{x}{5} - 2\left(\frac{x}{4} - \frac{x}{6}\right) = 22.$$

Multiply by 60 the L. C. D. of the fractions.

$$20x + 12x - 30x + 20x = 60 \times 22.$$

Combining, $22x = 60 \times 22$,

$$\therefore x = 60.$$

The required number, therefore, is 60.

1. The difference between the fifth and seventh parts of a certain number is 2. Find the number.

2. One-half of a certain number exceeds the sum of its fifth and seventh parts by 11. Find the number.

3. The sum of the third and sixth parts of a certain number exceeds the difference of its sixth and ninth parts by 16. Find the number.

4. There are two consecutive numbers, x and $x+1$, such that one-half the larger exceeds one-third the smaller number by 10. Find the numbers.

Exercise 56.

Ex. The sum of two numbers is 63, and if the greater is divided by the smaller number, the quotient is 2 and the remainder 3. Find the numbers.

Let $x =$ the greater number.

Then $63 - x =$ the smaller number.

$$\text{Since the quotient} = \frac{\text{Dividend} - \text{Remainder}}{\text{Divisor}},$$

and since, in this problem, the dividend is x, the remainder is 3, and the divisor is $63 - x$, we have

$$\frac{x-3}{63-x} = 2.$$

Solving, $$x = 43.$$

The two numbers, therefore, are 43 and 20.

1. The sum of two numbers is 100, and if the greater is divided by the smaller number, the quotient is 4 and the remainder 5. Find the numbers.

2. The sum of two numbers is 124, and if the greater is divided by the smaller number, the quotient is 4 and the remainder 4. Find the numbers.

3. The difference of two numbers is 49, and if the greater is divided by the smaller, the quotient is 4 and the remainder 4. Find the numbers.

4. The difference of two numbers is 91, and if the greater is divided by the smaller, the quotient is 8 and the remainder 7. Find the numbers.

5. Divide 320 into two parts such that the smaller part is contained in the larger part 11 times, with a remainder of 20.

Exercise 57.

Ex. Eight years ago a boy was one-fourth as old as he will be one year hence. How old is he now?

Let $x =$ the number of years old he is now.

Then $x - 8 =$ the number of years old he was eight years ago,

and $x + 1 =$ the number of years old he will be one year hence.

$$\therefore x - 8 = \tfrac{1}{4}(x + 1).$$

Solving, $x = 11.$

Therefore the boy is 11 years old.

1. A son is one-fourth as old as his father. In 24 years he will be one-half as old. Find the age of the son.

2. B's age is one-sixth of A's age. In 15 years B's age will be one-third of A's age. Find their ages.

3. The sum of the ages of A and B is 30 years, and 5 years hence B's age will be one-third of A's. Find their ages.

4. A father is 35 years old, and his son is one-fourth of that age. In how many years will the son be half as old as his father?

5. A is 60 years old, and B's age is two-thirds of A's. How many years ago was B's age one-fifth of A's?

6. A son is one-third as old as his father. Four years ago he was only one-fourth as old as his father. What is the age of each?

7. A is 50 years old, and B is half as old as A. In how many years will B be two-thirds as old as A?

8. B is one-half as old as A. Ten years ago he was one-fourth as old as A. What are their present ages?

9. The sum of the ages of a father and his son is 80 years. The son's age increased by 5 years is one-fourth of the father's age. Find their ages.

Exercise 58.

Ex. A can do a piece of work in 2 days, and B can do it in 3 days. How long will it take both together to do the work?

Let x = the number of days it will take both together.

Then $\frac{1}{x}$ = *the part both together can do in one day,*

$\frac{1}{2}$ = the part A can do in one day,

$\frac{1}{3}$ = the part B can do in one day,

and $\frac{1}{2}+\frac{1}{3}$ = *the part both together can do in one day.*

$$\therefore \frac{1}{2}+\frac{1}{3}=\frac{1}{x}.$$

Solving, $x = 1\frac{1}{5}$.

Therefore they together can do the work in $1\frac{1}{5}$ days.

1. A can do a piece of work in 3 days, B in 5 days, and C in 6 days. How long will it take them to do it working together?

2. A can do a piece of work in 5 days, B in 4 days, and C in 3 days. How long will it take them together to do the work?

3. A can do a piece of work in $2\frac{1}{2}$ days, B in $3\frac{1}{2}$ days, and C in $3\frac{3}{4}$ days. How long will it take them together to do the work?

4. A can do a piece of work in 10 days, B in 12 days; A and B together, with the help of C, can do the work in 4 days. How long will it take C alone to do the work?

5. A and B together can mow a field in 10 hours, A and C in 12 hours, and A alone in 20 hours. In what time can B and C together mow the field?

6. A and B together can build a wall in 12 days, A and C in 15 days, B and C in 20 days. In what time can they build the wall if they all work together?

HINT. By working 2 *days each* they build $\frac{1}{12} + \frac{1}{15} + \frac{1}{20}$ of it.

Exercise 59.

Ex. A cistern can be filled by three pipes in 15, 20, and 30 hours, respectively. In what time will it be filled by all the pipes together?

Let x = the number of hours it will take all together.

Then $\frac{1}{x}$ = the part all together can fill in one hour.

$\frac{1}{15}+\frac{1}{20}+\frac{1}{30}$ = the part all together can fill in one hour.

$$\frac{1}{15}+\frac{1}{20}+\frac{1}{30}=\frac{1}{x}.$$

Solving, $$x=6\tfrac{2}{3}.$$

Therefore the pipes together can fill it in $6\frac{2}{3}$ hours.

1. A cistern can be filled by three pipes in 16, 24, and 32 hours, respectively. In what time will it be filled by all the pipes together?

2. A tank can be filled by two pipes in 3 hours and 4 hours, respectively, and can be emptied by a third pipe in 6 hours. In what time will the cistern be filled if the pipes are all running together?

3. A tank can be filled by three pipes in 1 hour and 40 minutes, 3 hours and 20 minutes, and 5 hours, respectively. In what time will the tank be filled if all three pipes are running together?

4. A cistern can be filled by three pipes in $2\frac{1}{3}$ hours, $3\frac{1}{2}$ hours, and $4\frac{2}{3}$ hours, respectively. In what time will the cistern be filled if all the pipes are running together?

5. A cistern has three pipes. The first pipe will fill the cistern in 12 hours, the second in 20 hours, and all three pipes together will fill it in 6 hours. How long will it take the third pipe alone to fill it?

Exercise 60.

Ex. A courier who travels 6 miles an hour is followed, after 2 hours, by a second courier who travels $7\frac{1}{2}$ miles an hour. In how many hours will the second courier overtake the first?

Let $x =$ the number of hours the first travels.

Then $x - 2 =$ the number of hours the second travels,

$6x =$ the number of miles the first travels,

and $(x-2)7\frac{1}{2} =$ the number of miles the second travels.

They both travel the same distance.

$$\therefore 6x = (x-2)7\tfrac{1}{2},$$

or

$$12x = 15x - 30.$$

$$\therefore x = 10.$$

Therefore the second courier will overtake the first in $10 - 2$, or 8 hours.

1. A sets out from Boston and walks towards Portland at the rate of 3 miles an hour. Three hours afterward B sets out from the same place and walks in the same direction at the rate of 4 miles an hour. How far from Boston will B overtake A?

2. A courier who goes at the rate of $6\frac{1}{2}$ miles an hour is followed, after 4 hours, by another who goes at the rate of $7\frac{1}{2}$ miles an hour. In how many hours will the second overtake the first?

3. A person walks to the top of a mountain at the rate of two miles an hour, and down the same way at the rate of 4 miles an hour. If he is out 6 hours, how far is it to the top of the mountain?

4. In going a certain distance, a train travelling at the rate of 40 miles an hour takes 2 hours less than a train travelling 30 miles an hour. Find the distance.

Exercise 61.

Ex. A hare takes 4 leaps to a greyhound's 3; but 2 of the greyhound's leaps are equivalent to 3 of the hare's. The hare has a start of 50 leaps. How many leaps must the greyhound take to catch the hare?

Let $3x =$ the number of leaps taken by the greyhound.

Then $4x =$ the number of leaps of the hare in the same time.

Also, let $a =$ the number of feet in one leap of the hare.

Then $\frac{3a}{2} =$ the number of feet in one leap of the hound.

Therefore, $3x x \frac{3a}{2}$ or $\frac{9ax}{2}$ = the whole distance.

As the hare has a start of 50 leaps, and takes $4x$ leaps more before she is caught, and as each leap is a feet,

$$(50 + 4x)a = \text{the whole distance.}$$

$$\therefore \frac{9ax}{2} = (50 + 4x)a.$$

Multiply by 2, $$9ax = (100 + 8x)a,$$

Divide by a, $$9x = 100 + 8x,$$

$$x = 100,$$

$$\therefore 3x = 300.$$

Therefore the greyhound must take 300 leaps.

1. A hound makes 3 leaps while a rabbit makes 5; but 1 of the hound's leaps is equivalent to 2 of the rabbit's. The rabbit has a start of 120 leaps. How many leaps will the rabbit take before she is caught?

2. A rabbit takes 6 leaps to a dog's 5, and 7 of the dog's leaps are equivalent to 9 of the rabbit's. The rabbit has a start of 60 of her own leaps. How many leaps must the dog take to catch the rabbit?

3. A dog makes 4 leaps while a rabbit makes 5; but 3 of the dog's leaps are equivalent to 4 of the rabbit's. The rabbit has a start of 90 of the *dog's leaps*. How many leaps will each take before the rabbit is caught?

Exercise 62.

Ex. Find the time between 2 and 3 o'clock when the hands of a clock are together.

At 2 o'clock the hour-hand is 10 minute-spaces ahead of the minute-hand.

Let x = *the number of spaces the minute-hand moves over.*

Then $x - 10$ = the number of spaces the hour-hand moves over.

Now, as the minute-hand moves 12 times as fast as the hour-hand,

$12(x - 10)$ = *the number of spaces the minute-hand moves over.*

$$\therefore 12(x - 10) = x,$$

and

$$11x = 120.$$

$$\therefore x = 10\tfrac{10}{11}.$$

Therefore the time is $10\frac{10}{11}$ minutes past 2 o'clock.

1. Find the time between 5 and 6 o'clock when the hands of a clock are together.

2. Find the time between 2 and 3 o'clock when the hands of a clock are at right angles to each other.

HINT. In this case the minute-hand is 15 minutes ahead of the hour-hand.

3. Find the time between 2 and 3 o'clock when the hands of a clock point in opposite directions.

HINT. In this case the minute-hand is 30 minutes ahead of the hour-hand.

4. Find the time between 1 and 2 o'clock when the hands of a clock are at right angles to each other.

5. Find the time between 1 and 2 o'clock when the hands of a clock point in opposite directions.

6. At what time between 7 and 8 o'clock are the hands of a watch together?

Exercise 63.

Ex. A rectangle has its length 6 feet more and its width 5 feet less than the side of its equivalent square. Find the dimensions of the rectangle.

Let $x =$ the number of feet in a side of the square.

Then $x + 6 =$ the number of feet in the length of the rectangle,

and $x - 5 =$ the number of feet in the width of the rectangle.

Since the area of a rectangle is equal to the product of the number of units of length in the length and width of the rectangle,

$(x + 6)(x - 5) =$ the area of the rectangle in square feet,

and $x \times x =$ the area of the square in square feet.

But these areas are equal.

$$\therefore (x + 6)(x - 5) = x^2.$$

Solving, $x = 30.$

Therefore the dimensions of the rectangle are 36 feet and 25 feet.

1. A rectangle has its length and breadth respectively 7 feet longer and 6 feet shorter than the side of the equivalent square. Find its area.

2. The length of a floor exceeds the breadth by 5 feet. If each dimension were 1 foot more, the area of the floor would be 42 sq. ft. more. Find its dimensions.

3. A rectangle whose length is 6 feet more than its breadth, would have its area 35 sq. ft. more, if each dimension were 1 foot more. Find its dimensions.

4. The length of a rectangle exceeds its width by 3 feet. If the length is increased by 3 feet and the width diminished by 2 feet, the area will not be altered. Find its dimensions.

5. The length of a floor exceeds its width by 10 feet If each dimension were 2 feet more, the area would be 144 sq. ft. more. Find its dimensions.

143. Formulas and Rules. When the *given* numbers of a problem are represented by letters, the result obtained from solving the problem is a general expression which includes all problems of that class. Such an expression is called a **formula**, and the translation of this formula into words is called a **rule**.

144. We will illustrate by examples.

1. The sum of two numbers is s, and their difference d. Find the numbers.

Let $x =$ the smaller number;

then $x + d =$ the larger number.

Hence $x + x + d = s$,

or $2x = s - d$.

$$\therefore x = \frac{s-d}{2},$$

and
$$x + d = \frac{s-d}{2} + d = \frac{s-d+2d}{2},$$
$$= \frac{s+d}{2}.$$

Therefore the numbers are $\dfrac{s+d}{2}$ and $\dfrac{s-d}{2}$.

As these formulas hold true whatever numbers s and d stand for, we have the general rule for finding two numbers when their sum and difference are given:

Add the difference to the sum and take half the result for the greater number.

Subtract the difference from the sum and take half the result for the smaller number.

2. If A can do a piece of work in a days, and B can do the same work in b days, in how many days can both together do it?

Let $x =$ the required number of days.

Then, $\dfrac{1}{x} =$ *the part both together can do in one day.*

Now $\qquad \frac{1}{a}$ = the part A can do in one day,

and $\qquad \frac{1}{b}$ = the part B can do in one day,

therefore $\quad \frac{1}{a}+\frac{1}{b}$ = *the part both together can do in one day*

$$\frac{1}{a}+\frac{1}{b}=\frac{1}{x}.$$

Whence
$$x=\frac{ab}{a+b}.$$

The translation of this formula gives the following rule for finding the time required by two agents together to produce a given result when the time required by each agent separately is known.

Divide the product of the numbers which express the units of time required by each to do the work by the sum of these numbers, the quotient is the time required by both together.

145. Interest Formulas. The elements involved in computation of interest are the *principal*, *rate*, *time*, *interest*, and *amount*.

Let p = the principal,

r = the interest of $1 for 1 year, at the given rate,

t = the time expressed in years,

i = the interest for the given time and rate,

a = the amount (sum of principal and interest).

146. Given the Principal, Rate, and Time. Find the Interest.

Since r is the interest of \$1 for 1 year, pr is the interest of \$$p$ for 1 year, and prt is the interest of \$$p$ for t years

$$i = prt. \qquad \text{(Formula 1.)}$$

RULE. *Find the product of the principal, rate, and time.*

147. Given the Interest, Rate, and Time. Find the Principal.

By formula 1, $prt = i.$

Divide by rt, $p = \dfrac{i}{rt}.$ (Formula 2.)

RULE. *Divide the interest by the product of the rate and time.*

148. Given the Amount, Rate, and Time. Find the Principal.

From formula 1, $p + prt = a,$

or $p(1 + rt) = a.$

Divide by $1 + rt$, $p = \dfrac{a}{1 + rt}.$ (Formula 3.)

RULE. *Divide the amount by 1 plus the product of the rate and time.*

149. Given the Amount, Principal, and Rate. Find the Time.

From formula 1, $p + prt = a.$

Transpose p, $prt = a - p.$

Divide by pr, $t = \frac{a-p}{pr}.$ (Formula 4.)

RULE. *Subtract the principal from the amount, and divide the result by the product of the principal and rate.*

150. Given the Amount, Principal, and Time. Find the Rate.

From formula 1, $p + prt = a.$

Transpose p, $prt = a - p.$

Divide by pt, $r = \frac{a-p}{pt}.$ (Formula 5.)

RULE. *Subtract the principal from the amount, and divide the result by the product of the principal and time.*

Exercise 64.

Solve the following examples by the preceding formulas:

1. The sum of two angles is $120° \, 30' \, 30''$ and their difference $59° \, 30' \, 30''$. Find the angles.

2. Find the interest of \$1000 for 3 years and 4 months at 4%.

3. Find the principal that will amount to \$2280 in 3 years and 6 months at 4%.

4. Find the principal that will produce \$280 interest in 2 years and 4 months at 3%.

5. Find the principal that will produce \$270 interest in 1 year and 6 months at 6%.

6. Find the principal that will amount to \$590 in 4 years at $4\frac{1}{2}\%$.

7. Find the rate if the amount of \$250 for 4 years is \$300.

8. Find the rate if \$1000 amounts to \$2000 in 16 years and 8 months.

9. Find the time required for the interest on \$400 to be \$54 at $4\frac{1}{2}\%$.

10. Find the time required for \$160 to amount to \$250 at 6%.

11. How much money must be invested at 5% to yield an annual income of \$1250?

12. Find the principal that will produce \$100 a month if invested at 6% per annum.

13. Find the rate if the interest on \$1000 for 8 months is \$40.

14. Find the time for a sum of money on interest at 5% to double itself.

CHAPTER XI.

SIMULTANEOUS EQUATIONS OF THE FIRST DEGREE.

151. If we have two unknown numbers and but one relation between them, we can find an unlimited number of pairs of values for which the given relation will hold true. Thus, if x and y are unknown, and we have given only the one relation $x + y = 10$, we can *assume* any value for x, and then from the relation $x + y = 10$ find the corresponding value of y. For from $x + y = 10$ we find $y = 10 - x$. If x stands for 1, y stands for 9; if x stands for 2, y stands for 8; if x stands for -2, y stands for 12; and so on without end.

152. We may, however, have two equations that express *different* relations between the two unknown numbers. Such equations are called **independent equations**. Thus, $x+y = 10$ and $x - y = 2$ are independent equations, for they evidently express *different* relations between x and y.

153. Independent equations involving the *same* unknown numbers are called **simultaneous equations**.

If we have two unknown numbers, and two independent equations involving them, there is but *one* pair of values which will hold true for both equations. Thus, if besides the relation $x + y = 10$, we have also the relation $x - y = 2$, the only pair of values for which both equations will hold true is the pair $x = 6$, $y = 4$.

Observe that in this problem x stands for the same number in *both* equations; so also does y.

154. Simultaneous equations are solved by combining the equations so as to obtain a single equation with one unknown number.

This process is called **Elimination.**

155. Elimination by Addition or Subtraction.

1. Solve:

$$5x - 3y = 20 \tag{1}$$
$$2x + 5y = 39 \tag{2}$$

Multiply (1) by 5, and (2) by 3,

$$25x - 15y = 100 \tag{3}$$
$$6x + 15y = 117 \tag{4}$$

Add (3) and (4), $31x \qquad = 217$

$$\therefore x = 7.$$

Substitute the value of x in (2),

$$14 + 5y = 39.$$
$$5y = 25.$$
$$\therefore y = 5.$$

In this solution y is eliminated by *addition.*

2. Solve:

$$6x + 35y = 177 \tag{1}$$
$$8x - 21y = 33 \tag{2}$$

Multiply (1) by 4, and (2) by 3,

$$24x + 140y = 708 \quad (3)$$

$$24x - 63y = 99 \quad (4)$$

Subtract,

$$203y = 609$$

$$\therefore y = 3.$$

Substitute the value of y in (2),

$$8x - 63 = 33.$$

$$8x = 96.$$

$$\therefore x = 12.$$

In this solution x is eliminated by *subtraction.*

156. To eliminate by addition or subtraction, therefore,

Multiply the equations by such numbers as will make the coefficients of one of the unknown numbers equal in the resulting equations.

Add the resulting equations if these equal coefficients have unlike signs; subtract one from the other if these equal coefficients have like signs.

NOTE. It is generally best to select the letter to be eliminated which requires the smallest multipliers to make its coefficients equal; and the smallest multiplier for each equation is found by dividing the L. C. M. of the coefficients of this letter by the given coefficient in that equation. Thus, in example 2, the L. C. M. of 6 and 8 (the coefficients of x) is 24, and hence the smallest multipliers of the two equations are 4 and 3, respectively.

Sometimes the solution is simplified by first adding the given equations, or by subtracting one from the other.

Ex.
$$x + 49y = 51 \quad (1)$$
$$49x + y = 99 \quad (2)$$
Add (1) and (2), $50x + 50y = 150$ (3)

Divide (3) by 50, $x + y = 3.$ (4)

Subtract (4) from (1), $48y = 48.$

$\therefore y = 1.$

Subtract (4) from (2), $48x = 96.$

$\therefore x = 2.$

Exercise 65.

Solve by addition or subtraction:

1. $\left.\begin{aligned} 5x + 4y &= 14 \\ 17x - 3y &= 31 \end{aligned}\right\}$

2. $\left.\begin{aligned} 3x - 2y &= 5 \\ 2x + 5y &= 16 \end{aligned}\right\}$

3. $\left.\begin{aligned} 2x - 3y &= 7 \\ 5x + 2y &= 27 \end{aligned}\right\}$

4. $\left.\begin{aligned} 7x + 6y &= 20 \\ 2x + 5y &= 9 \end{aligned}\right\}$

5. $\left.\begin{aligned} x + 5y &= 11 \\ 3x + 2y &= 7 \end{aligned}\right\}$

6. $\left.\begin{aligned} 3x - 5y &= 13 \\ 4x - 7y &= 17 \end{aligned}\right\}$

7. $\left.\begin{aligned} 8x - y &= 3 \\ 7x + 2y &= 63 \end{aligned}\right\}$

8. $\left.\begin{aligned} 5x - 4y &= 7 \\ 7x + 3y &= 70 \end{aligned}\right\}$

9. $\left.\begin{aligned} x + 21y &= 2 \\ 2x + 27y &= 19 \end{aligned}\right\}$

10. $\left.\begin{aligned} 6x - 13y &= -1 \\ 5x - 12y &= -2 \end{aligned}\right\}$

11. $\left.\begin{aligned} 7x + y &= 265 \\ 3x - 5y &= 5 \end{aligned}\right\}$

12. $\left.\begin{aligned} 2x + 3y &= 7 \\ 8x - 5y &= 11 \end{aligned}\right\}$

13. $\left.\begin{aligned} 5x + 7y &= 19 \\ 7x + 4y &= 15 \end{aligned}\right\}$

14. $\left.\begin{aligned} 11x - 12y &= 9 \\ 4x + 5y &= 22 \end{aligned}\right\}$

15. $\left.\begin{aligned} x + 8y &= 17 \\ 7x - 3y &= 1 \end{aligned}\right\}$

16. $\left.\begin{aligned} 4x + 3y &= 25 \\ 5x - 4y &= 8 \end{aligned}\right\}$

Clear of fractions and solve:

17. $\left.\begin{aligned} \frac{2x}{3} - \frac{5y}{4} &= 3 \\ \frac{7x}{4} - \frac{5y}{3} &= \frac{43}{3} \end{aligned}\right\}$

18. $\left.\begin{aligned} \frac{7x}{6} + \frac{6y}{7} &= 32 \\ \frac{5x}{4} - \frac{2y}{3} &= 1 \end{aligned}\right\}$

19. $\left.\begin{aligned} \frac{x+y}{4} - \frac{7x-5y}{11} &= 3 \\ \frac{x}{5} - \frac{2y}{7} + 1 &= 0 \end{aligned}\right\}$

20. $\left.\begin{aligned} \frac{6x+7y}{2} &= 22 \\ \frac{55y-2x}{5} &= 20 \end{aligned}\right\}$

21. $\left.\begin{aligned} \frac{x+y}{2} - \frac{x-y}{3} &= 8 \\ \frac{x+y}{3} + \frac{x-y}{4} &= 11 \end{aligned}\right\}$

22. $\left.\begin{aligned} \frac{8x-5y}{7} + \frac{11y-4x}{5} &= 4 \\ \frac{17x-13y}{5} + \frac{2x}{3} &= 7 \end{aligned}\right\}$

23. $$\left.\begin{aligned}\frac{5x-3y}{3}+\frac{7x-5y}{11}&=4\\ \frac{15y-3x}{7}+\frac{7y-3x}{5}&=4\end{aligned}\right\}$$

24. $$\left.\begin{aligned}\frac{2x-3}{4}-\frac{y-8}{5}&=\frac{y+3}{4}\\ \frac{x-7}{3}+\frac{4y+1}{11}&=3\end{aligned}\right\}$$

25. $$\left.\begin{aligned}\frac{x-2y}{6}-\frac{x+3y}{4}&=\frac{3}{2}\\ \frac{2x-y}{6}-\frac{3x+y}{4}&=\frac{5y}{4}\end{aligned}\right\}$$

26. $$\left.\begin{aligned}\frac{x}{a+b}+\frac{y}{a-b}&=\frac{1}{a-b}\\ \frac{x}{a+b}-\frac{y}{a-b}&=\frac{1}{a+b}\end{aligned}\right\}$$

NOTE. To find x in problem 26, add the equations; to find y, subtract one from the other. Do not clear of fractions.

157. Problems involving Two Unknown Numbers.

Ex. If A gives B \$10, B will have three times as much money as A. If B gives A \$10, A will have twice as much money as B. How much has each?

Let $\quad x =$ the number of dollars A has,

and $\quad y =$ the number of dollars B has.

Then, after A gives B \$10,

$$x - 10 = \text{the number of dollars A has,}$$
$$y + 10 = \text{the number of dollars B has.}$$

Since B's money is now 3 times A's, we have,

$$y + 10 = 3(x - 10). \tag{1}$$

If B gives A \$10,

$$x + 10 = \text{the number of dollars A has,}$$
$$y - 10 = \text{the number of dollars B has.}$$

Since A's money is now 2 times B's, we have

$$x + 10 = 2(y - 10). \tag{2}$$

From the solution of equations (1) and (2), $x = 22$, and $y = 26$.

Therefore A has \$22, and B has \$26.

Exercise 66.

1. If A gives B \$200, A will then have half as much money as B; but if B gives A \$200, B will have one-third as much as A. How much has each?

2. Half the sum of two numbers is 20, and three times their difference is 18. Find the numbers.

3. The sum of two numbers is 36, and their difference is equal to one-eighth of the smaller number increased by 2. Find the numbers.

4. If 4 yards of velvet and 3 yards of silk are sold for \$33, and 5 yards of velvet and 6 yards of silk for \$48, what is the price per yard of the velvet and of the silk?

5. If 7 bushels of wheat and 10 of rye are sold for \$15, and 4 bushels of wheat and 5 of rye are sold for \$8, what is the price per bushel of the wheat and of the rye?

6. If 12 pounds of tea and 4 pounds of coffee cost \$7, and 4 pounds of tea and 12 pounds of coffee cost \$5, what is the price per pound of tea and of coffee?

7. Six horses and 7 cows can be bought for \$1000, and 11 horses and 13 cows for \$1844. Find the value of a horse and of a cow.

Exercise 67.

Ex. A certain fraction becomes equal to $\frac{1}{2}$ if 2 is added to its numerator, and equal to $\frac{1}{3}$ if 3 is added to its denominator. Find the fraction.

Let $$\frac{x}{y} = \text{the required fraction.}$$

Then $$\frac{x+2}{y} = \frac{1}{2},$$

and $$\frac{x}{y+3} = \frac{1}{3}.$$

The solution of these equations gives 7 for x, and 18 for y.

Therefore the required fraction is $\frac{7}{18}$.

1. If the numerator of a certain fraction is increased by 2 and its denominator diminished by 2, its value will be 1. If the numerator is increased by the denominator and the denominator is diminished by 5, its value will be 5. Find the fraction.

2. If 1 is added to the denominator of a fraction, its value will be $\frac{1}{2}$. If 2 is added to its numerator, its value will be $\frac{3}{5}$. Find the fraction.

3. If 1 is added to the numerator of a fraction, its value will be $\frac{1}{5}$. If 1 is added to its denominator, its value will be $\frac{1}{7}$. Find the fraction.

4. If the numerator of a fraction is doubled and its denominator diminished by 1, its value will be $\frac{1}{2}$. If its denominator is doubled and its numerator increased by 1, its value will be $\frac{1}{7}$. Find the fraction.

5. In a certain proper fraction the difference between the numerator and the denominator is 15. If the numerator is multiplied by 4 and the denominator increased by 6, its value will be 1. Find the fraction.

Exercise 68.

The expression 64 means $60+4$, that is, 10 *times* $6+4$, and has for its *digits* 6 and 4. If the digits were unknown and represented by x and y, the number would be represented by $10x+y$.

Ex. The sum of the two digits of a number is 10, and if 18 is added to the number, the digits will be reversed. Find the number.

Let $x =$ the tens' digit,

and $y =$ the units' digit.

Then $10x + y =$ the number.

Hence $x + y = 10,$ (1)

and $10x + y + 18 = 10y + x.$ (2)

From (2), $9x - 9y = -18,$

or $x - y = -2.$ (3)

Add (1) and (3), $2x = 8,$

and therefore $x = 4.$

Subtract (3) from (1), $2y = 12,$

and therefore $y = 6.$

Therefore the number is 46.

1. The sum of the two digits of a number is 9, and if 9 is added to the number, the digits will be reversed. Find the number.

2. A certain number of two digits is equal to eight times the sum of its digits, and if 45 is subtracted from the number, the digits will be reversed. Find the number.

3. The sum of a certain number of two digits and the number formed by reversing the digits is 132, and the difference of these numbers is 18. Find the numbers.

4. The sum of the two digits of a number is 9, and if the number is divided by the sum of its digits, the quotient is 6. Find the number.

Exercise 69.

Ex. A sum of money, at simple interest, amounted to \$2480 in 4 years, and to \$2600 in 5 years. Find the sum and the rate of interest.

Let $x =$ the number of dollars in the principal,

and $y =$ the rate of interest.

The interest for one year is $\frac{y}{100}$ of the principal; that is, $\frac{xy}{100}$. For 4 years the interest is $\frac{4xy}{100}$, and for 5 years $\frac{5xy}{100}$. The amount is principal + interest,

or
$$x + \frac{4xy}{100} = 2480.$$
$$x + \frac{5xy}{100} = 2600.$$

Hence
$$100x + 4xy = 248,000. \quad (1)$$
$$100x + 5xy = 260,000. \quad (2)$$

Divide (1) by 4 and (2) by 5, and we have

$$25x + xy = 62,000$$
$$20x + xy = 52,000$$

Subtract, $$5x = 10,000.$$

Therefore $$x = 2000.$$

Substitute the value of x in (1), $y = 6$.

Therefore the sum is \$2000, and the rate 6

1. A sum of money, at simple interest, amounted in 5 years to \$3000, and in 6 years to \$3100. Find the sum and the rate of interest.

2. A sum of money, at simple interest, amounted in 10 months to \$1680, and in 18 months to \$1744. Find the sum and the rate of interest.

3. A man has \$10,000 invested, a part at 4%, and the remainder at 5%. The annual income from his 4% investment is \$40 more than from his 5% investment. Find the sum invested at 4% and at 5%.

Exercise 70.

Miscellaneous Examples.

1. Half the sum of two numbers is 20; and 5 times their difference is 20. Find the numbers.

2. A certain number when divided by a second number gives 7 for a quotient and 4 for a remainder. If three times the first number is divided by twice the second number, the quotient is 11 and the remainder 4. Find the numbers.

3. A fraction becomes $\frac{4}{5}$ in value by the addition of 2 to its numerator and 3 to its denominator. If 2 is subtracted from its numerator and 1 from its denominator, the value of the fraction is $\frac{3}{4}$. Find the fraction.

4. A farmer sold 50 bushels of wheat and 30 of barley for 74 dollars; and at the same prices he sold 30 bushels of wheat and 50 bushels of barley for 70 dollars. What was the price of the wheat and of the barley per bushel?

5. If A gave $10 to B, he would then have three times as much money as B; but if B gave $5 to A, A would have four times as much as B. How much has each?

6. A and B have together $100. If A were to spend one-half of his money, and B one-third of his, they would then have only $55 between them. How much money has each?

7. A fruit-dealer sold 6 lemons and 3 oranges for 21 cents, and 3 lemons and 8 oranges for 30 cents. What was the price of each?

8. If A gives me 10 apples, he will have just twice as many as B. If he gives the 10 apples to *B* instead of to me, A and B will each have the same number. How many apples has each?

CHAPTER XII.

QUADRATIC EQUATIONS.

158. An equation which contains the *square* of the unknown number, but no higher power, is called a **quadratic equation**.

159. A quadratic equation which involves but one unknown number as x, can contain only:

1. Terms involving the square of x.
2. Terms involving the first power of x.
3. Terms which do not involve x.

Collecting similar terms, every quadratic equation can be made to assume the form

$$ax^2 + bx + c = 0,$$

where a, b, and c are known numbers, and x the unknown number.

If a, b, c are numbers expressed by figures, the equation is a **numerical quadratic**. If a, b, c are numbers represented wholly or in part by letters, the equation is a **literal quadratic**.

160. In the equation $ax^2 + bx + c = 0$, a, b, and c are called the **coefficients** of the equation. The third term, c, is called the **constant term**.

If the first power of x is wanting, the equation is a **pure quadratic**; in this case $b = 0$.

If the first power of x is present, the equation is an **affected** or **complete quadratic**.

Pure Quadratic Equations.

161. Examples.

1. Solve the equation $5x^2 - 48 = 2x^2$.

We have	$5x^2 - 48 = 2x^2.$
Collect the terms,	$3x^2 = 48.$
Divide by 3,	$x^2 = 16.$
Extract the square root,	$x = \pm 4.$

The sign $\pm$ before the 4, read *plus or minus*, shows that the root is either + or −. For $(+4) \times (+4) = 16$, and $(-4) \times (-4) = 16$

The square root of any number is positive or negative. Hitherto we have given only the positive value. In this chapter we shall give both values. This sign $\sqrt{}$, called the **radical sign**, is used to indicate that a root is to be extracted. Thus $\sqrt{4}$ means the square root of 4 is required. $\sqrt[3]{4}$ means the third root of 4 is required; the small figure placed over the radical sign is called the **index** of the root, and shows the root required.

2. Solve the equation $3x^2 - 15 = 0$.

We have	$3x^2 = 15,$
or	$x^2 = 5.$
Extract the square root,	$x = \pm\sqrt{5}.$

The roots cannot be found exactly, since the square root of 5 cannot be found exactly; it can, however, be determined approximately to any required degree of accuracy; for example, the roots lie between 2.23606 and 2.23607; and between −2.23606 and −2.23607.

3. Solve the equation $3x^2 + 15 = 0$.

We have $$3x^2 = -15,$$

or $$x^2 = -5.$$

Extract the square root, $$x = \pm\sqrt{-5}.$$

There is no square root of a negative number, since the square of any number, positive or negative, is positive; $(-5) \times (-5) = +25$.

The square root of −5 differs from the square root of +5 in that the latter can be found as accurately as we please, while the former cannot be found at all.

162. A root which can be found exactly is called an **exact** or **rational** root. Such roots are either whole numbers or fractions.

A root which is indicated but can be found only approximately is called a **surd**. Such roots involve the roots of imperfect powers.

Rational and surd roots are together called **real** roots.

A root which is indicated but cannot be found, either exactly or approximately, is called an **imaginary** root. Such roots involve the even roots of negative numbers.

Exercise 71.

Solve:

1. $5x^2 - 2 = 3x^2 + 6.$

2. $3x^2 + 1 = 2x^2 + 10.$

3. $4x^2 - 50 = x^2 + 25.$

4. $(x - 6)(x + 6) = 28.$

5. $(x - 5)(x + 5) = 24.$

6. $3(x^2 - 11) + 2(x^2 - 5) = 82.$

7. $11(x^2 + 5) + 6(3 - x^2) = 198.$

8. $5x^2 + 3 - 2(17 - x^2) = 32.$

9. $4(x + 1) - 4(x - 1) = x^2 - 1.$

10. $86 - 52x = 2(8 - x)(2 - 3x).$

11. Find two numbers that are to each other as 3 to 4, and the difference of whose squares is 112.

HINT. Let $3x$ stand for the smaller and $4x$ for the larger number.

12. A boy bought a number of oranges for 36 cents. The price of an orange was to the number bought as 1 to 4. How many oranges did he buy, and how many cents did each orange cost?

13. A certain street contains 144 square rods, and the length is 16 times the width. Find the width.

14. Find the number of rods in the length, and in the width of a rectangular field containing $3\frac{3}{5}$ acres, if the length is 4 times the width.

Affected Quadratic Equations.

163. Since

$$(x + b)^2 = x^2 + 2bx + b^2, \quad \text{and} \quad (x - b)^2 = x^2 - 2bx + b^2,$$

it is evident that the expression $x^2 + 2bx$ or $x^2 - 2bx$ lacks only the *third term*, b^2, of being a perfect square.

This third term is the square of half the coefficient of x.

Every affected quadratic may be made to assume the form $x^2 + 2bx = c$ or $x^2 - 2bx = c$, by dividing the equation through by the coefficient of x^2.

To **solve** such an equation:

The first step is to add to both members *the square of half the coefficient of* x. This is called *completing the square.*

The second step is to *extract the square root* of each member of the resulting equation.

The third step is to *reduce* the two resulting simple equations.

1. Solve the equation $x^2 - 8x = 20$.

We have $\quad x^2 - 8x = 20.$

Complete the square, $\quad x^2 - 8x + 16 = 36.$

Extract the square root, $\quad x - 4 = \pm 6.$

Reduce, using the upper sign, $x = 4 + 6 = 10,$

or using the lower sign, $x = 4 - 6 = -2.$

The roots are 10 and -2.

Verify by putting these numbers for x in the given equation.

$x = 10,$	$x = -2,$
$10^2 - 8(10) = 20,$	$(-2)^2 - 8(-2) = 20,$
$100 - 80 = 20.$	$4 + 16 = 20.$

2. Solve the equation $\dfrac{x+1}{x-1} = \dfrac{4x-3}{x+9}.$

Free from fractions, $(x+1)(x+9) = (x-1)(4x-3).$

Therefore, $-3x^2 + 17x = -6.$

Since the square root of a negative number cannot be taken, the coefficient of x^2 must be changed to $+$.

Divide by -3, $x^2 - \frac{17}{3}x = 2.$

Half the coefficient of x is $\frac{1}{2}$ of $-\frac{17}{3} = -\frac{17}{6}$, and the square of $-\frac{17}{6}$ is $\frac{289}{36}$. Add the square of $-\frac{17}{6}$ to both sides, and we have

$$x^2 - \frac{17x}{3} + \left(\frac{17}{6}\right)^2 = 2 + \frac{289}{36}.$$

Now $$2 + \frac{289}{36} = \frac{72}{36} + \frac{289}{36} = \frac{361}{36},$$

therefore, $$x^2 - \tfrac{17}{3}x + \left(\frac{17}{6}\right)^2 = \frac{361}{36}.$$

Extract the root, $x - \frac{17}{6} = \pm\frac{19}{6}$.

Reduce, $x - \frac{17}{6} = \pm\frac{19}{6}$.

$$\therefore x = \frac{17}{6} + \frac{19}{6} = \frac{36}{6} = 6,$$

or $x = \frac{17}{6} - \frac{19}{6} = -\frac{2}{6} = -\frac{1}{3}$.

The roots are 6 and $-\frac{1}{3}$.

Verify by putting these numbers for x in the original equation.

$x = 6.$	$x = -\frac{1}{3}$
$\frac{6+1}{6-1} = \frac{24-3}{6+9}.$	$\frac{-\frac{1}{3}+1}{-\frac{1}{3}-1} = \frac{-\frac{4}{3}-3}{-\frac{1}{3}+9}.$
$\frac{7}{5} = \frac{21}{15}$	$-\frac{2}{4} = -\frac{13}{26}.$
$\frac{7}{5} = \frac{7}{5}$	

Exercise 72.

Solve:

1. $x^2 - 12x + 27 = 0.$

2. $x^2 - 6x + 8 = 0.$

3. $x^2 - 4 = 4x - 7.$

4. $5x^2 - 4x - 1 = 0.$

5. $4x - 3 = 2x - x^2.$

6. $9x^2 - 24x + 16 = 0.$

7. $6x^2 - 5x - 1 = 0.$

8. $4x + 3 = x^2 + 2x.$

9. $16x^2 - 16x + 3 = 0.$

10. $3x^2 - 10x + 3 = 0.$

11. $x^2 - 14x - 51 = 0.$

12. $34x - x^2 - 225 = 0.$

13. $x^2 + x - 20 = 0.$

14. $x^2 - x - 12 = 0.$

15. $2x^2 - 12x = -10.$

16. $3x^2 + 12x - 36 = 0.$

17. $(2x-1)^2 + 9 = 6(2x-1).$

18. $6(9x^2 - x) = 55(x^2 - 1).$

19. $32 - 3x^2 - 10x = 0.$

20. $9x^2 - 6x - 143 = 0.$

21. $\dfrac{x}{x-1} - \dfrac{x-1}{x} = \dfrac{3}{2}.$

22. $\dfrac{1}{x-2} + \dfrac{2}{x+2} = \dfrac{5}{6}.$

23. $\dfrac{5x+7}{x-1} = 3x + 11.$

24. $\dfrac{7}{x+4} - \dfrac{1}{4-x} = \dfrac{2}{3}.$

25. $\dfrac{2}{x+3} + \dfrac{x+3}{2} = \dfrac{10}{3}.$

26. $\dfrac{2x}{x+2} + \dfrac{x+2}{2x} = 2.$

27. $\dfrac{3(x-1)}{x+1} - \dfrac{2(x+1)}{x-1} = 5.$

28. $\dfrac{2x+5}{2x-5} = \dfrac{7x-5}{2x}.$

29. $\dfrac{3x-1}{4x+7} = \dfrac{x+1}{x+7}.$

30. $\dfrac{2x-1}{x+3} = \dfrac{x+3}{2x-1}.$

31. $\dfrac{x+4}{x-4} - \dfrac{x+2}{x-3} = 1.$

32. $\dfrac{4}{x-1} - \dfrac{5}{x+2} = \dfrac{1}{2}.$

33. $\dfrac{2}{x-1} = \dfrac{3}{x-2} + \dfrac{2}{x-4}.$

34. $\dfrac{5}{x-2} - \dfrac{3}{x-1} = \dfrac{1}{2}.$

35. $\dfrac{x}{7-x} + \dfrac{7-x}{x} = \dfrac{29}{10}.$

36. $\dfrac{2x-1}{x-1} + \dfrac{1}{6} = \dfrac{2x-3}{x-2}.$

164. Problems involving Quadratics. Problems which involve quadratic equations apparently have two solutions, since a quadratic equation has two roots.

When both roots of the quadratic equation are positive integers, they will, in general, both be admissible solutions. Fractional and negative roots will in some problems give admissible solutions; in other problems they will not give admissible solutions.

The reason that every root of the equation will not always satisfy the conditions of the problem is that the problem may have certain restrictions, expressed or implied, that cannot be expressed in the equation.

No difficulty will be found in selecting the result which belongs to the particular problem we are solving. Sometimes, by a change in the statement of the problem, we may form a new problem which corresponds to the result that was inapplicable to the original problem.

Here as in simple equations x stands for an unknown *number*.

1. The sum of the squares of two consecutive numbers is 41. Find the numbers.

Let $x =$ one number,

and $x + 1 =$ the other.

Then $x^2 + (x+1)^2 =$ the sum of the squares;

but $41 =$ the sum of the squares.

$$\therefore x^2 + (x+1)^2 = 41.$$
$$x^2 + x^2 + 2x + 1 = 41.$$
$$2x^2 + 2x = 40.$$
$$x^2 + x = 20.$$

The solution of this equation gives $x = 4$, or -5.

The positive root 4 gives for the numbers 4 and 5.

The negative root -5 is inapplicable to the problem, as *consecutive numbers* are understood to be integers which follow each other in the common scale: 1, 2, 3, 4 . . . .

2. In a certain nest seven times the number of birds in the nest is equal to twice the square of the number increased by 3. Find the number.

Let $\quad x =$ the number of birds.

Then $\quad 7x = 7$ times the number

and $\quad 2x^2 + 3 =$ twice the square of the number plus 3.

As these two expressions are equal we have

$$2x^2 + 3 = 7x.$$

The solution of this *equation* gives $x = 3$ or $x = \frac{1}{2}$.

The value $\frac{1}{2}$ is not applicable to the *problem* for the number of birds must be a whole number.

3. A cistern has two pipes. By one of them it can be filled 6 hours sooner than by the other, and by both together in 4 hours. Find the time it will take each pipe alone to fill it.

Let $\quad x =$ the number of hours it takes the smaller pipe.

Then $\quad x - 6 =$ the number of hours it takes the larger pipe.

Therefore $\quad \frac{1}{x} + \frac{1}{x-6} =$ the part both can fill in one hour.

But $\quad \frac{1}{4} =$ the part both can fill in one hour.

$$\frac{1}{x} + \frac{1}{x-6} = \frac{1}{4}$$

The solution of this *equation* gives $x = 12$ or $x = 2$.

The value 2 is not applicable to the *problem.*

Therefore it takes one pipe 12 hr. and the other 6 hr.

4. A rug is 1 yard longer than it is broad. The number of sq. yds. in the rug is 12. Find its length and breadth.

Let $\quad x =$ the number of yards in the breadth.

Then $\quad x + 1 =$ the number of yards in the length

and $\quad x(x + 1) =$ the number of sq yds in the rug.

Hence $\quad x(x + 1) = 12.$

The solution of this equation gives $x = 3$ or $x = -4$.

The dimensions are therefore 3 yards and 4 yards.

Exercise 73.

1. Find two numbers whose sum is 11, and whose product is 30.

2. Find two numbers whose difference is 10, and the sum of whose squares is 250.

3. A man is five times as old as his son, and the square of the son's age diminished by the father's age is 24. Find their ages.

4. A number increased by its square is equal to nine times the next higher number. Find the number.

5. The square of the sum of any two consecutive numbers lacks 1 of being twice the sum of the squares of the numbers. Show that this statement is true.

6. The length of a rectangular court exceeds its breadth by 2 rods. If the length and breadth were each increased by 3 rods, the area of the court would be 80 square rods. Find the dimensions of the court.

7. The area of a certain square will be doubled, if its dimensions are increased by 6 feet and 4 feet respectively. Find its dimensions.

8. The perimeter of a rectangular floor is 76 feet and the area of the floor is 360 square feet. Find the dimensions of the floor.

9. The length of a rectangular court exceeds its breadth by 2 rods, and its area is 120 square rods. Find the dimensions of the court.

10. The combined ages of a father and son amount to 64 years. Twice the father's age exceeds the square of the son's age by 8 years. Find their respective ages.

Exercise 74.

Ex. A boat sails 30 miles at a uniform rate. If the rate had been 1 mile an hour more, the time of the sailing would have been 1 hour less. Find the rate of the sailing.

Let $x =$ the rate in miles per hour.

Then $\frac{30}{x} =$ the number of hours.

On the other supposition the rate would have been $x + 1$ miles an hour and the time $\frac{30}{x+1}$.

Hence $\frac{30}{x} - \frac{30}{x+1} =$ the difference in hours for the sailing.

But $1 =$ the difference in hours for the sailing.

$$\frac{30}{x} - \frac{30}{x+1} = 1.$$

The solution of this equation gives $x = 5$, or $x = -6$.

Therefore, the rate of the sailing is 5 miles an hour.

1. A boat sails 30 miles at a uniform rate. If the rate had been 1 mile an hour less, the time of the sailing would have been 1 hour more. Find the rate of the sailing.

2. A laborer built 35 rods of stone wall. If he had built 2 rods less each day, it would have taken him 2 days longer. How many rods did he build a day on the average?

3. A man bought flour for $30. Had he bought 1 barrel more for the same sum, the flour would have cost him $1 less per barrel. How many barrels did he buy?

4. A man bought some knives for $6. Had he bought 2 less for the same money, he would have paid 25 cents more for each knife. How many knives did he buy?

5. What number exceeds its square root by 30?

HINT. Let x^2 denote the number.

CHAPTER XIII.

ARITHMETICAL PROGRESSION.

165. A series of numbers is said to form an **Arithmetical Progression** if the difference between any term and the preceding term is the same throughout the series.

Thus a, b, c, d, etc., are in arithmetical progression if $b-a$, $c-b$, $d-c$, etc., are all equal.

166. This difference is called the **common difference** of the progression, and is represented by d. If d is positive, the progression is an *increasing* series; if d is negative, the progression is a *decreasing* series.

What is the common difference in each of the following series?

$$\begin{array}{rrrrl} 1, & 4, & 7, & 10, & \dots \\ 5, & 7, & 9, & 11, & \dots \\ 10, & 9, & 8, & 7, & \dots \\ 7, & 3, & -1, & -5, & \dots \end{array}$$

167. If the first term of an arithmetical progression is represented by a and the common difference by d, then

the *second* term will be $a + d$,
the *third* term will be $a + 2d$,
the *fourth* term will be $a + 3d$,

and so on, the coefficient of d in each term being always less by 1 than the *number of the term.*

Hence the nth term will be $a + (n - 1)d$.

If we represent the nth term by l, we have

$$l = a + (n - 1)d. \qquad \text{Formula (1)}$$

168. We can, therefore, find any term of an arithmetical progression if the first term and common difference are given, or if any *two* terms are given.

1. Find the 10th term of an arithmetical progression if the 1st term is 3 and the common difference is 4.

By formula (1), the 10th term is $3 + (10 - 1)4$, or 39.

2. If the 8th term of an arithmetical progression is 25, and the 23d term 70, find the series.

By formula (1), the 23d term is $a + 22d$,
and the 8th term is $a + 7d$.

Therefore, $a + 22d = 70$
and $a + 7d = 25$.

Subtract, $15d = 45$

and $d = 3,$

whence $a = 4.$

The series is therefore 4, 7, 10, 13, etc.

169. Arithmetical Mean. If three numbers are in arithmetical progression, the middle number is called the arithmetical mean of the other two numbers.

If a, A, b are in arithmetical progression, A is the arithmetical mean of a and b. Hence, by the definition of an arithmetical series,

$$A - a = b - A,$$

whence $$A = \frac{a+b}{2}.$$ Formula (2)

Hence, the arithmetical mean of any two numbers is found by taking half their sum.

170. Sometimes it is required to insert several arithmetical means between two numbers.

If m = the number of means, and n = the whole number of terms, then $m + 2 = n$. If $m + 2$ is substituted for n in formula (1),

$$l = a + (n - 1)d,$$

the result is $$l = a + (m + 1)d.$$

By transposing a, $l - a = (m+1)d.$

$$\therefore \frac{l-a}{m+1} = d. \qquad \text{Formula (3)}$$

Thus, if it be required to insert six means between 3 and 17, the value of d is found to be $\frac{17-3}{6+1} = 2$; and the series will be 3, 5, 7, 9, 11, 13, 15, 17.

Exercise 75.

1. Find the 25th term in the series 3, 6, 9, ...

2. Find the 13th term in the series 50, 49, 48, ...

3. Find the 15th term in the series $\frac{1}{7}, \frac{3}{7}, \frac{5}{7}, \ldots$.

4. Find the 19th term in the series $\frac{1}{4}, -\frac{1}{4}, -\frac{3}{4}, \ldots$.

5. Find the 10th term in an arithmetical progression whose 1st term is 5 and 3d term 9.

6. Find the 11th term in an arithmetical progression whose 1st term is 10 and whose 6th term is 5.

7. If the 3d term of an arithmetical progression is 20 and the 13th term is 100, what is the 20th term?

8. Which term of the series 5, 7, 9, 11, ..., is 43?

9. Which term of the series $\frac{4}{3}, \frac{3}{2}, \frac{5}{3}, \ldots$, is 18?

10. What is the arithmetical mean of 20 and 32?

11. What is the arithmetical mean of $a+b$ and $a-b$?

12. Insert 8 arithmetical means between 20 and 29.

171. To Find the Sum of Any Number of Terms of an Arithmetical Series.

If l denote the last term, a the first term, n the number of terms, d the common difference, and s the sum of the terms, it is evident that the series beginning with the first term will be a, $a+d$, $a+2d$, etc., and beginning with the last term will be l, $l-d$, $l-2d$, etc. Therefore,

$$\begin{array}{rcl} s &=& a + (a+d) + (a+2d) + \ldots + (l-d) + l, \quad \text{or} \\ s &=& l + (l-d) + (l-2d) + \ldots + (a+d) + a \\ \hline 2s &=& (a+l) + (a+l) + (a+l) + \ldots + (a+l) + (a+l) \end{array}$$

$2s = (a+l)$ taken as many times as there are *terms*,

$$2s = n(a+l),$$

$$\text{and } s = \frac{n}{2}(a+l). \qquad \text{Formula (4)}$$

Putting for l its value $a+(n-1)d$, in formula (4), we have

$$s = \frac{n}{2}\{a + a + (n-1)d\}$$

$$= \frac{n}{2}\{2a + (n-1)d\} \qquad \text{Formula (5)}$$

1. Find the sum of the first 16 terms of the series 5, 7, 9, 11.

Here $\qquad a = 5, \quad d = 2, \quad n = 16.$

Putting these values in formula (5) we have

$$\begin{aligned} s &= \tfrac{16}{2}(10 + 15 \times 2) \\ &= 320 \end{aligned}$$

2. Show that the sum of any number of odd numbers, beginning with 1, is a square number.

The series of odd numbers is 1, 3, 5, 7, ...

Here $a = 1$ and $d = 2$.

Putting these values in formula (5) we have

$$\begin{aligned} s &= \frac{n}{2}\{2 + (n-1)2\} \\ &= \frac{n}{2} \times 2n \\ &= n^2. \end{aligned}$$

Therefore the sum of the first 5 odd numbers is 5^2 or 25, of the first 8 odd numbers is 8^2 or 64, and so on.

3. The sum of 20 terms of an arithmetical progression is 420, and the first term is 2. Find the common difference.

Here $s = 420$, $n = 20$, and $a = 2$.

Putting these values in formula (5), we have

$$\begin{aligned} 420 &= \tfrac{20}{2}(4 + 19d) \\ &= 40 + 190d \\ 190d &= 380 \\ \therefore d &= 2. \end{aligned}$$

Therefore the common difference is 2.

Exercise 76.

1. Find the sum of 3, 5, 7, ..., to 20 terms.

2. Find the sum of 14, $14\frac{1}{2}$, 15, ..., to 12 terms.

3. Find the sum of $\frac{7}{6}$, 1, $\frac{5}{6}$, ..., to 10 terms.

4. Find the sum of -7, -5, -3, ..., to 16 terms.

5. Find the sum of 12, 9, 6, ..., to 21 terms.

6. Find the sum of $-10\frac{1}{2}$, -9, $-7\frac{1}{2}$, ..., to 25 terms.

7. The sum of three numbers in arithmetical progression is 9, and the sum of their squares is 35. Find the numbers.

HINT. Let $x - y$, x, $x + y$, stand for the numbers.

8. A common clock strikes the hours from 1 to 12. How many times does it strike every 24 hours?

9. The Greenwich clock strikes the hours from 1 to 24. How many times does it strike in 24 hours?

10. In a potato race each man picked up 50 potatoes placed in line a yard apart, and the first potato one yard from the basket, picking up one potato at a time and bringing it to the basket. How many yards did each man run, the start being made from the basket?

11. A heavy body falling from a height falls 16.1 feet the first second, and in each succeeding second 32.2 feet more than in the second next preceding. How far will a body fall in 19 seconds?

12. A stone dropped from a bridge reached the water in just 3 seconds. Find the height of the bridge. (See Ex. 11.)

13. The arithmetical mean between two numbers is 13, and the mean between the double of the first and the triple of the second is $33\frac{1}{2}$. Find the numbers.

14. Find three numbers of an arithmetical series whose sum shall be 27, and the sum of the first and second shall be $frac45$ of the sum of the second and third.

15. A travels uniformly 20 miles a day; B travels 8 miles the first day, 12 the second, and so on, in arithmetical progression. If they start Monday morning from the same place and travel in the same direction, how far apart will they be Saturday night?

16. The sum of three terms of an arithmetical progression is 36, and the square of the mean exceeds the product of the other two terms by 49. Find the numbers.

CHAPTER XIV.

GEOMETRICAL PROGRESSION.

172. A series of numbers is said to be in **Geometrical Progression** when the quotient of any term divided by the preceding term is the same throughout the series.

Thus a, b, c, d, etc., are in geometrical progression if $\frac{b}{a} = \frac{c}{b} = \frac{d}{c}$, etc.

173. This quotient is called the **common ratio**, and is represented by r.

State the common ratio of the following series:

$$\begin{array}{rrrrr} 1, & 3, & 9, & 27, & \ldots \\ 2, & 4, & 8, & 16, & \ldots \\ 16, & 8, & 4, & 2, & \ldots \\ \frac{2}{3}, & 1, & \frac{3}{2}, & \frac{9}{4}, & \ldots \\ 4, & -2, & 1, & -\frac{1}{2}, & \ldots \end{array}$$

174. If the first term of a geometrical progression is represented by a, and the common ratio by r, then

the *second* term will be ar,
the *third* term will be ar^2,
the *fourth* term will be ar^3,

and so on, the index of r being always less by 1 than the *number of the term in the series.*

Hence the nth term will be ar^{n-1}.

If we denote the nth term by l, we have

$$l = ar^{n-1}. \qquad \text{Formula (1)}$$

175. If the first term and common ratio are given, or if any *two terms* are given, we can find the series.

1. Find the 5th term of a geometrical progression if the first is 3 and the common ratio 2.

In formula (1), put 5 for n, 3 for a, and 2 for r.

Then $$l = 3 \times 2^4 = 48.$$

Therefore the 5th term is 48.

2. Find the geometrical series if the 5th term is 48 and the 7th term is 192.

The 5th and 7th terms are ar^4 and ar^6, respectively.

Whence $$ar^4 = 48, \qquad (1)$$

and $$ar^6 = 192. \qquad (2)$$

Divide (2) by (1), $$r^2 = 4.$$

$$\therefore r = \pm 2.$$

From (1), $$a = \tfrac{48}{16} = 3.$$

Therefore the series is 3, ±6, 12, ±24, ...

176. Geometrical Mean. If three numbers are in geometrical progression, the middle number is called the *geometrical mean* of the other two numbers. Hence, if a, G, b are in geometrical progression, G is the geometrical mean of a and b.

By the definition of a geometrical progression,

$$\frac{G}{a} = \frac{b}{G}.$$

$$\therefore G^2 = ab,$$

and $$G = \pm\sqrt{ab}. \qquad \text{Formula (2)}$$

Hence, *the geometrical mean of any two numbers is the square root of their product.*

177. To Find the Sum of Any Number of Terms of a Geometrical Progression.

If l denote the last term, a the first term, n the number of terms, r the common ratio, and s the sum of the n terms, then

$$s = a + ar + ar^2 + ar^3 + \cdots + ar^{n-1}.$$

Multiply by r, $$rs = ar + ar^2 + ar^3 + \cdots + ar^{n-1} + ar^n.$$

Therefore, by subtracting the first equation from the second,

$$rs - s = ar^n - a,$$

or $$(r-1)s = a(r^n - 1).$$

$$\therefore s = \frac{a(r^n-1)}{r-1}. \qquad \text{Formula (3)}$$

178. When r is < 1, this formula will be more convenient if written

$$s = \frac{a(1 - r^n)}{1 - r}.$$

1. Find the sum of 8 terms of the series

$$1, \quad 2, \quad 4, \quad \ldots.$$

Here $a = 1, \quad r = 2, \quad n = 8.$

From formula (3), $s = 1(2^8 - 1) = 255.$

2. Find the sum of 6 terms of the series

$$2, \quad 3, \quad \tfrac{9}{2}, \quad \ldots.$$

Here $a = 2, \quad r = \tfrac{3}{2}, \quad n = 6.$

From formula (3),
$$\begin{aligned} s &= \frac{2\{(\frac{3}{2})^6 - 1\}}{\frac{3}{2} - 1} \\ &= \frac{2\{\frac{729}{64} - 1\}}{\frac{1}{2}} \\ &= \frac{4\{729 - 64\}}{64} \\ &= 41\tfrac{9}{16}. \end{aligned}$$

Exercise 77.

1. Find the 5th term of 3, 9, 27, ...

2. Find the 7th term of 3, 6, 12, ...

3. Find the 8th term of 6, 3, $\frac{3}{2}$, ...

4. Find the 9th term of 1, −2, 4, ...

5. Find the geometrical mean between 2 and 8.

6. Find the common ratio if the 1st and 3d terms are 2 and 32.

Find the sum of the series:

7. 3, 9, 27, ... to 6 terms.

8. 3, 6, 12, ... to 8 terms.

9. 6, 3, $\frac{3}{2}$, ... to 7 terms.

10. 8, 4, 2, ... to 8 terms.

11. 64, 32, 16, ... to 9 terms.

12. 64, −32, 16, ... to 5 terms.

13. $\frac{1}{2}$, $\frac{1}{3}$, $\frac{2}{9}$, ... to 4 terms.

14. If a blacksmith uses seven nails in putting a shoe on a horse's foot, and receives 1 cent for the first nail, 2 cents for the second nail, and so on, what does he receive for putting on the shoe?

15. If a boy receives 2 cents for his first day's work, 4 cents for his second day, 8 cents for the third day, and so on for 12 days, what will his wages amount to?

16. If the population of a city is $10,000$, and increases 10% a year for four years, what will be its population at the end of the four years? (Here $l = ar^4$.)

CHAPTER XV.

SQUARE AND CUBE ROOTS.

Square Roots of Compound Expressions.

179. Since the square of $a+b$ is $a^2+2ab+b^2$, the square root of $a^2+2ab+b^2$ is $a+b$.

It is required to find a method of extracting the root $a+b$ when $a^2+2ab+b^2$ is given.

Ex. The first term, a, of the root is obviously the square root of the first term, a^2, in the expression.

$$\begin{array}{r|l} a^2 + 2ab + b^2 & a+b \\ a^2 & \\ \hline 2a + b \quad 2ab + b^2 & \\ 2ab + b^2 & \\ \hline \end{array}$$

If the a^2 is subtracted from the given expression, the remainder is $2ab+b^2$. Therefore the second term, b, of the root is obtained when the first term of this remainder is divided by $2a$; that is, by *double the part of the root already found.* Also, since

$$2ab+b^2=(2a+b)b,$$

the divisor is *completed by adding to the trial-divisor the new term of the root.*

Ex. Find the square root of $25x^2 - 20x^3y + 4x^4y^2$.

$$
\begin{array}{lll}
 & 25x^2 - 20x^3y + 4x^4y^2 & \underline{|\,5x - 2x^2y} \\
\text{Here } a^2 = (5x)^2 = & 25x^2 & \\
2a + b = 10x - 2x^2y & -20x^3y + 4x^4y^2 & \\
 & -20x^3y + 4x^4y^2 &
\end{array}
$$

The expression is *arranged* according to the ascending powers of x.

The square root of the first term is $5x$, hence $5x$ is the first term of the root. $(5x)^2$ or $25x^2$ is subtracted, and the remainder is

$$-20x^3y + 4x^4y^2.$$

The second term of the root, $-2x^2y$, is obtained by dividing $-20x^3y$ by $10x$, the double of $5x$, and this new term of the root is also annexed to the divisor, $10x$, to complete the divisor.

180. The same method will apply to longer expressions, if care be taken to obtain the *trial-divisor* at each stage of the process, *by doubling the part of the root already found*, and to obtain the *complete divisor by annexing the new term of the root to the trial-divisor.*

Ex. Find the square root of

$$1 + 10x^2 + 25x^4 + 16x^6 - 24x^5 - 20x^3 - 4x.$$

$$
\begin{array}{r|l|l}
 & 16x^6 - 24x^5 + 25x^4 - 20x^3 + 10x^2 - 4x + 1 & \underline{4x^3 - 3x^2 + 2x - 1} \\
 & 16x^6 & \\
\hline
8x^3 - 3x^2 & -24x^5 + 25x^4 & \\
 & -24x^5 + 9x^4 & \\
\hline
8x^3 - 6x^2 + 2x & 16x^4 - 20x^3 + 10x^2 & \\
 & 16x^4 - 12x^3 + 4x^2 & \\
\hline
8x^3 - 6x^2 + 4x - 1 & -8x^3 + 6x^2 - 4x + 1 & \\
 & -8x^3 + 6x^2 - 4x + 1 & \\
\hline
\end{array}
$$

The expression is arranged according to the descending powers of x.

It will be noticed that each successive trial-divisor may be obtained by taking the preceding complete divisor with its *last term doubled.*

Exercise 78.

Find the square root of: **1.** $a^2 + 2ab + 2ac + b^2 + 2bc + c^2$.

2. $x^4 + 2x^3 + 3x^2 + 2x + 1$.

3. $x^4 - 4x^3y + 6x^2y^2 - 4xy^3 + y^4$.

4. $4a^4 - 12a^3b + 29a^2b^2 - 30ab^3 + 25b^4$.

5. $16x^6 + 24x^5y + 9x^4y^2 - 16x^3y^3 - 12x^2y^4 + 4y^6$.

6. $4x^6 - 4x^4y^2 + 12x^3y^3 + x^2y^4 - 6xy^5 + 9y^6$.

181. Arithmetical Square Roots. In the general method of extracting the square root of a number expressed by figures, the first step is to mark off the figures into *groups*.

Since $1 = 1^2$, $100 = 10^2$, $10,000 = 100^2$, and so on, it is evident that the square root of a number between 1 and 100 lies between 1 and 10; of a number between 100 and 10,000 lies between 10 and 100. In other words, the square root of a number expressed by *one* or *two* figures is a number of *one* figure, of a number expressed by *three* or *four* figures is a number of *two* figures, and so on.

If, therefore, an integral square number is divided into groups of two figures each, from the right to the left, the number of figures in the root will be equal to the number of groups of figures. The last group to the left may have only one figure.

Ex. Find the square root of 3249.

$$\begin{array}{r|l} & 3249\ (57 \\ & \underline{25} \\ 107\,) & 749 \\ & \underline{749} \end{array}$$

In this case, a in the typical form $a^2 + 2ab + b^2$ represents 5 tens, that is, 50, and b represents 7. The 25 subtracted is really 2500, that is, a^2, and the complete divisor $2a + b$ is $2 \times 50 + 7 = 107$.

182. The same method will apply to numbers of more than two groups of figures by considering a in the typical form to represent at each step *the part of the root already found.*

It must be observed that a *represents so many tens with respect to the next figure of the root.*

Ex. Find the square root of 94, 249.

$$\begin{array}{r|l} & 9\,42\,49\,(307 \\ & 9 \\ \hline 607) & 4249 \\ & 4249 \\ \hline \end{array}$$

NOTE. Since the first trial divisor, 60, is not contained in 42, we put a zero in the root, and bring down the next group, 49.

183. If the square root of a number has decimal places, the number itself will have *twice* as many. Thus, if 0.21 is the square root of some number, this number will be $(0.21)^2 = 0.21 \times 0.21 = 0.0441$, and if 0.111 be the root, the number will be $(0.111)^2 = 0.111x0.111 = 0.012321$.

Therefore, the number of *decimal* places in every square decimal will be *even*, and the number of decimal places in the root will be *half* as many as in the given number itself.

Hence, if a given number contain a decimal, we divide it into groups of two figures each, by beginning at the decimal point and marking toward the left for the integral number, and toward the right for the decimal. We must have the last group on the right of the decimal point contain *two* figures, annexing a cipher when necessary.

Ex. Find the square roots of 41.2164 and 965.9664.

```
      41.21 64 (6.42               9 65.96 64 (31.08
      36                           9
 124) 521                       61)65
      496                          61
1282)2564                     6208)49664
     2564                          49664
```

184. If a number contain an *odd* number of decimal places, or if any number give a *remainder* when as many figures in the root have been obtained as the given number has groups, then its exact square root cannot be found. We may, however, approximate to its exact root as near as we please by annexing ciphers and continuing the operation.

The square root of a common fraction whose denominator is not a perfect square can be found approximately by reducing the fraction to a decimal and then extracting the root; or by reducing the fraction to an equivalent fraction whose denominator is a perfect square, and extracting the square root of both terms of the fraction.

1. Find the square roots of 3 and 357.357.

```
       3. (1.732...                3 57. 35 70 (18.903...
       1                           1
 27) 2 00                    28) 2 57
     1 89                        2 24
343) 11 00                  369) 33 35
     10 29                       33 21
3462) 71 00               37803) 14 70 00
      69 24                      11 34 09
```

2. Find the square root of $\frac{5}{8}$.

Since $$\frac{5}{8} = 0.625,$$

the square root of $$\frac{5}{8} = \sqrt{0.625}$$ $$= 0.79057.$$

Or, $$\frac{5}{8} = \frac{10}{16},$$

and the square root of $$\frac{5}{8} = \frac{\sqrt{10}}{\sqrt{16}} = \tfrac{1}{4}\sqrt{10}$$ $$= \tfrac{1}{4}(3.16227)$$ $$= 0.79057.$$

Exercise 79.

Find the square root of:

1. 324.

2. 441.

3. 529.

4. 961.

5. 10.24.

6. 53.29.

7. 53, 824.

8. 616, 225.

9. 1, 500, 625.

10. 346, 921.

11. 31, 371, 201.

12. 1, 522, 756.

Find to four decimal places the square root of:

13. 2.

14. 3.

15. 5.

16. 6.

17. 0.5.

18. 0.9.

19. $\frac{2}{3}$.

20. $\frac{3}{4}$.

21. $\frac{4}{5}$.

22. $\frac{5}{8}$.

Cube Roots of Compound Expressions.

185. Since the cube of $a+b$ is $a^3+3a^2b+3ab^2+b^3$, the cube root of a$^3 + 3a^2b + 3ab^2 + b^3$ is $a + b$.

It is required to devise a method for extracting the cube root $a + b$ when $a^3 + 3a^2b + 3ab^2 + b^3$ is given.

1. Find the cube root of $a^3 + 3a^2b + 3ab^2 + b^3$.

$$
\begin{array}{lll}
 & a^3 + 3a^2b + 3ab^2 + b^3 & \underline{|\, a + b} \\
3a^2 & a^3 & \\
\quad +3ab + b^2 & 3a^2b + 3ab^2 + b^3 & \\
\hline
3a^2 + 3ab + b^2 & 3a^2b + 3ab^2 + b^3 & \\
\end{array}
$$

The first term a of the root is obviously the cube root of the first term a^3 of the given expression.

If a^3 be subtracted, the remainder is $3a^2b + 3ab^2 + b^3$; therefore, the second term b of the root is obtained by dividing the first term of this remainder by *three times the square of* a.

Also, since $3a^2b + 3ab^2 + b^3 = (3a^2 + 3ab + b^2)b$, the *complete divisor* is obtained by adding $3ab + b^2$ to the *trial divisor* $3a^2$.

2. Find the cube root of $8x^3 + 36x^2y + 54xy^2 + 27y^3$.

$$\begin{array}{rr|l|l}
 & & 8x^3 + 36x^2y + 54xy^2 + 27y^3 & 2x + 3y \\
 & 12x^2 & 8x^3 & \\
(6x+3y)3y = & 18xy + 9y^2 & 36x^2y + 54xy^2 + 27y^3 & \\
\hline
 & 12x^2 + 18xy + 9y^2 & 36x^2y + 54xy^2 + 27y^3 &
\end{array}$$

The cube root of the first term is $2x$, and this is therefore the first term of the root. $8x^3$, the cube of $2x$, is subtracted.

The second term of the root, $3y$, is obtained by dividing $36x^2y$ by $3(2x)^2 = 12x^2$, which corresponds to $3a^2$ in the typical form, and the divisor is completed by annexing to $12x^2$ the expression

$$\{3(2x) + 3y\}3y = 18xy + 9y^2,$$

which corresponds to $3ab + b^2$ in the typical form.

186. The same method may be applied to longer expressions by considering a in the typical form $3a^2 + 3ab + b^2$ to represent at each stage of the process *the part of the root already found.* Thus, if the part of the root already found is $x + y$, then $3a^2$ of the typical form will be represented by $3(x+y)^2$; and if the third term of the root be $+z$, then $3ab+b^2$ will be represented by $3(x+y)z+z^2$. So that the complete divisor, $3a^2+3ab+b^2$, will be represented by $3(x+y)^2+3(x+y)z+z^2$.

Ex. Find the cube root of $x^6-3x^5+5x^3-3x-1$.

$$
\begin{array}{rr|l}
 & & \underline{x^2 - x - 1} \\
 & & x^6 - 3x^5 \qquad\qquad + 5x^3 - 3x - 1 \\
 & 3x^4 & x^6 \\
(3x^2-x)(-x) = & -3x^3 + x^2 & -3x^5 \qquad\qquad + 5x^3 \\
 & 3x^4 - 3x^3 + x^2 & -3x^5 + 3x^4 - x^3 \\
 & & \qquad -3x^4 + 6x^3 - 3x - 1 \\
3(x^2-x)^2 = & 3x^4 - 6x^3 + 3x^2 & \\
(3x^2-3x-1)(-1) = & -3x^2 + 3x + 1 & \\
 & 3x^4 - 6x^3 \qquad + 3x + 1 & \qquad -3x^4 + 6x^3 - 3x - 1
\end{array}
$$

NOTE. The root is placed *above* the given expression because there is no room for it on the page at the right of the expression.

The first term of the root, x^2, is obtained by taking the cube root of the first term of the given expression; and the first trial-divisor, $3x^4$, is obtained by taking three times the square of this term.

The next term of the root is found by dividing $-3x^5$, the first term of the remainder after x^6 is subtracted, by $3x^4$, and the first complete divisor, $3x^4-3x^3+x^2$, is found by annexing to the trial divisor $(3x^2-x)(-x)$, which expression corresponds to $(3a+b)b$ in the typical form.

The part of the root already found (a) is now represented by x^2-x, therefore $3a^2$ is represented by $3(x^2-x)^2=3x^4-6x^3+3x^2$, the second trial divisor, and $(3a+b)b$ by $(3x^2-3x-1)(-1)$, since b in this case is found to be -1, therefore, in the second complete divisor, $3a^2+(3a+b)b$ is represented by

$$(3x^4-6x^3+3x^2)+(3x^2-3x-1)(-1)=3x^4-6x^3+3x+1.$$

Exercise 80.

Find the cube root of

1. $x^3+3x^2y+3xy^2+y^3$.

2. $8x^3-12x^2+6x-1$.

3. $8x^3-36x^2y+54xy^2-27y^3$.

4. $64a^3-144a^2x+108ax^2-27x^3$.

5. $1+3x+6x^2+7x^3+6x^4+3x^5+x^6$.

6. $x^6-3x^5+6x^4-7x^3+6x^2-3x+1$.

187. Arithmetical Cube Roots. In extracting the cube root of a number expressed by figures, the first step is to mark it off into groups.

Since $1 = 1^3$, $1000 = 10^3$, $1,000,000 = 100^3$, and so on, it follows that the cube root of any number between 1 and 1000, that is, of any number which has *one*, *two*, or *three* figures, is a number of *one* figure, and that the cube root of any number between 1000 and $1,000,000$, that is, of any number which has *four*, *five*, or *six* figures, is a number of *two* figures, and so on.

If, therefore, an integral cube number be divided into groups of three figures each, from right to left, the number of figures in the root will be equal to the number of groups. The last group to the left may consist of one, two, or three figures.

188. If the cube root of a number have decimal places, the number itself will have *three times* as many. Thus, if 0.11 be the cube root of a number, the number is $0.11 \times 0.11x0.11 = 0.001331$. Hence, if a given number contain a decimal, we divide the figures of the number into groups of three figures each, by beginning at the decimal point and marking toward the left for the integral number, and toward the right for the decimal. We must be careful to have the last group on the right of the decimal point contain *three* figures, annexing ciphers when necessary.

Extract the cube root of 42875.

$$
\begin{array}{rrr|l}
 & & & 42\ 875\ (35 \\
 & & a^3 = & 27 \\
\cline{4-4}
3a^2 = & 3 \times 30^2 = & 2700 & 15\ 875 \\
3ab = & 3 \times (30 \times 5) = & 450 & \\
b^2 = & 5^2 = & 25 & \\
\cline{3-3}
 & & 3175 & 15\ 875 \\
\cline{4-4}
\end{array}
$$

Since 42875 has two groups, the root will have two figures.

The first group, 42, contains the cube of the tens of the root.

The greatest cube in 42 is 27, and the cube root of 27 is 3. Hence 3 is the tens' figure of the root.

We subtract 27 from 42, and bring down the next group, 875. Since a is 3 tens or 30, $3a^2 = 3 \times 30^2$, or 2700. This trial-divisor is contained 5 times in 15875. The trial-divisor is completed by adding $3ab + b^2$; that is, $450 + 25$, to the trial-divisor.

189. The same method will apply to numbers of more than two groups of figures, by considering in each case a, the part of the root already found, as so many tens with respect to the next figure of the root.

Extract the cube root of 57512456.

$$
\begin{array}{rrr|l}
 & & & 57\ 512\ 456\ (386 \\
 & & a^3 = & 27 \\ \cline{4-4}
3a^2 = & 3\times 30^2 = & 2700 & 30\ 512 \\
3ab = & 3\times(30\times 8) = & 720 & \\
b^2 = & 8^2 = & 64 & \\ \cline{3-3}
 & & 3484 & 27\ 872 \\ \cline{4-4}
 & & & 2\ 640\ 456 \\
3a^2 = & 3\times 380^2 = & 433200 & \\
3ab = & 3\times(380\times 6) = & 6840 & \\
b^2 = & 6^2 = & 36 & \\ \cline{3-3}
 & & 440076 & 2\ 640\ 456 \\ \cline{4-4}
\end{array}
$$

Extract the cube root of 187.149248.

$$
\begin{array}{rrr|l}
 & & & 187.149\ 248\ (5.72 \\
 & & a^3 = & 125 \\ \cline{4-4}
3a^2 = & 3\times 50^2 = & 7500 & 62\ 149 \\
3ab = & 3\times(50\times 7) = & 1050 & \\
b^2 = & 7^2 = & 49 & \\ \cline{3-3}
 & & 8599 & 60\ 193 \\ \cline{4-4}
 & & & 1\ 956\ 248 \\
3a^2 = & 3\times 570^2 = & 974700 & \\
3ab = & 3\times(570\times 2) = & 3420 & \\
b^2 = & 2^2 = & 4 & \\ \cline{3-3}
 & & 978124 & 1\ 956\ 248 \\ \cline{4-4}
\end{array}
$$

It will be seen from the groups of figures that the root will have one integral and two decimal places.

190. If the given number is not a perfect cube, ciphers may be annexed, and a value of the root may be found as near to the *true* value as we please.

Extract the cube root of 1250.6894.

$$\begin{array}{rrr|l}
 & & & 1\ 250.689\,400\ (10.77 \\
 & & a^3 = & 1 \\
3a^2 = & 3 \times 10^2 = & 300 & 250
\end{array}$$

Since 300 is not contained in 250, the next figure of the root will be 0.

$$\begin{array}{rrr|l}
3a^2 = & 3 \times 100^2 = & 30000 & 250\ 689 \\
3ab = & 3 \times (100 \times 7) = & 2100 & \\
b^2 = & 7^2 = & 49 & \\
\hline
 & & 32149 & 225\ 043 \\
\hline
 & & & 25\ 646\ 400 \\
3a^2 = & 3 \times 1070^2 = & 3434700 & \\
3ab = & 3 \times (1070 \times 7) = & 22470 & \\
b^2 = & 7^2 = & 49 & \\
\hline
 & & 3457219 & 24\ 200\ 533 \\
\hline
 & & & 1\ 445\ 867
\end{array}$$

191. Notice that if a denotes the first term, and b the second term of the root, the *first complete divisor* is

$$3a^2 + 3ab + b^2,$$

and the *second trial-divisor* is $3(a+b)^2$, that is,

$$3a^2 + 6ab + 3b^2.$$

This expression may be obtained by adding to the preceding complete divisor, $3a^2 + 3ab + b^2$, *its second term and twice its third term.* Thus:

$$\begin{array}{r}
3a^2 + 3ab + \ \ b^2 \\
3ab + 2b^2 \\
\hline
3a^2 + 6ab + 3b^2
\end{array}$$

This method of obtaining *trial-divisors* is of great importance for shortening numerical work, as may be seen in the following example:

Ex. Extract the cube root of 5 to five places of decimals.

$$\begin{array}{rrr|l}
 & & & 5.000\,(1.70997 \\
 & & a^3 = & 1 \\
\hline
3a^2 = & 3 \times 10^2 = & 300 & 4\,000 \\
3ab = & 3(10 \times 7) = & 210 & \\
b^2 = & 7^2 = & 49 & \\
 & & 559 & 3\,913 \\
\hline
 & & 259 & 87\,000\,000 \\
3a^2 = & 3 \times 1700^2 = & 8670000 & \\
3ab = & 3(1700 \times 9) = & 45900 & \\
b^2 = & 9^2 = & 81 & \\
 & & 8715981 & 78\,443\,829 \\
\hline
 & & 45981 & 8\,556\,1710 \\
3a^2 = & 3 \times 1709^2 = & 8762043 & 7\,885\,8387 \\
\hline
 & & & 670\,33230 \\
 & & & 613\,34301 \\
\hline
\end{array}$$

After the first two figures of the root are found, the next trial-divisor is obtained by bringing down 259, the sum of the 210 and 49 obtained in completing the preceding divisor, then *adding the three lines connected by the brace*, and annexing two ciphers to the result.

This trial divisor is 86,700, and if we add $3ab + b^2$ to complete the divisor, when $b = 1$, the complete divisor will be $86,700 + 511 = 87,211$, and this is larger than the dividend 87,000. We therefore put 0 for the next figure of the root. We then bring down another group and annex two more ciphers to the trial-divisor.

The last two figures of the root are found by division. The rule in such cases is, that two less than the number of figures already obtained may be found without error by division, the divisor being three times the square of the part of the root already found.

192. The cube root of a common fraction whose denominator is not a perfect cube can be found approximately by reducing the fraction to a decimal, and then extracting the root.

Exercise 81.

Find the cube root of:

1. 46,656.

2. 42,875.

3. 91,125.

4. 274,625.

5. 110,592.

6. 258,474,853.

7. 109,215,352.

8. 259,694,072.

9. 127,263,527.

10. 385,828,352.

11. 1879.080904.

12. 1838.265625.

Find to four decimal places the cube root of:

13. 0.01.	**16.** 4.	**19.** 2.5.	**22.** $\frac{2}{3}$.
14. 0.05.	**17.** 10.	**20.** 2.05.	**23.** $\frac{3}{4}$.
15. 0.2.	**18.** 87.	**21.** 3.02.	**24.** $\frac{9}{11}$.

ANSWERS.

Exercise 1. Page 12

1. 14.	**4.** 11.	**7.** 9.	**10.** 2.	**13.** 2.	**16.** 3.	**19.** 3.
2. 10.	**5.** 13.	**8.** 7.	**11.** 3.	**14.** 8.	**17.** 1.	**20.** 4.
3. 13.	**6.** 7.	**9.** 6.	**12.** 6.	**15.** 4.	**18.** 1.	**21.** 10.

Exercise 2. Page 14

1. 91. **2.** 21. **3.** 60. **4.** 24. **5.** 96. **6.** 16. **7.** 36.

8. $4a + 4b$.	**13.** $3ab - 3c$.	**18.** $3ab - 3ac$.
9. $4a - 4b$.	**14.** $3c - 3ab$.	**19.** $5ab^2 + 5ac$.
10. $2a^2 + 2b^2$.	**15.** $ab + ac$.	**20.** $5ab^2 - 5ac^2$.
11. $2a^2 - 2b^2$.	**16.** $ab - ac$.	
12. $3ab + 3c$.	**17.** $3ab + 3ac$.	**21.** $5a^2b^2 - 5a^2c$.

Exercise 3. Page 15

1. 63.	**6.** 1250.	**11.** 105.	**16.** 0.	**21.** 540.
2. 280.	**7.** 105.	**12.** 105.	**17.** 1800.	
3. 300.	**8.** 105.	**13.** 0.	**18.** 540.	
4. 98.	**9.** 315.	**14.** 135.	**19.** 0.	
5. 81.	**10.** 35.	**15.** 120.	**20.** 270.	

Exercise 4. Page 17

1. 21. **2.** 26. **3.** 72. **4.** 85. **5.** 30. **6.** 17. **7.** 8. **8.** 50. **9.** 24. **10.** 0. **11.** 12. **12.** 100. **13.** 80. **14.** 71. **15.** 139. **16.** 17. **17.** 8. **18.** 5. **19.** 3. **20.** 6. **21.** 5. **22.** 1. **23.** 2. **24.** 2.

Exercise 5. Page 17

1. a plus b; a minus b; a times b; a divided by b.

3. $a + b$.

5. $a - b$.

7. $x - y$.

9. $4x$; x^4.

11. $35 - x$.

12. $x - a$.

14. $14 - x$.

15. $a - x$.

17. xy.

18. $\frac{x}{y}$.

Exercise 6. Page 19

2. $\frac{a}{b}$.

4. $(x - 3)$ yr.; $(x + 7)$ yr.

6. $7(2x - y)$.

8. $x + 1$; $x - 1$.

9. $20 - d$.

11. $x + 8$.

13. $x - 10$.

14. 10.

Exercise 7. Page 20

1. $(40 - x)$ yr.

2. $(a + y)$ yr.

3. 4.

5. ab.

6. $5x - 3x$.

8. $2x - 3 - (x + 1)$.

9. 40.

10. 12.

11. $100a + 25b + 10c$.

12. $100 - x - y$.

14. $xy + c$.

Exercise 8. Page 21

2. $xy - a^2$.

3. $\frac{ph}{gk}$.

4. $6m^2 + 5c(d + b - a)$.

5. $5(2n + 1) - 6(c - a + b)$.

6. $\$100 - \$(a + b + 2c)$.

8. $\frac{1}{x}$.

9. $\frac{1}{x} + \frac{1}{y} + \frac{1}{z}$.

10. $n + (n + 1) + (n + 2)$; $n(n + 1)(n + 2)$.

11. $\frac{36}{x}$.

12. qd.

13. $qd + r$.

14. $2x$.

15. $\frac{10x}{12}$.

16. $\frac{6a}{b}$.

17. $4m$.

18. $x + 17$.

19. $x + y + c$.

20. $36x$.

21. $\frac{c}{4}$.

22. $x - 1$, x, $x + 1$.

23. $2n + 3$.

Exercise 9. Page 30

1. 4.

2. 5.

3. 3.

4. 1.

5. 13.

6. 0.

7. 5.

8. 5.

9. 7.

10. 4.

11. 4.

12. 1.

13. 25.

14. $32\frac{1}{2}$.

15. 6.

16. 10.

17. 3.

18. 1.

19. 7.

20. 13.

21. 12. **22.** 14. **23.** 7. **24.** 5. **25.** 0. **26.** 15. **27.** $10\frac{1}{2}$. **28.** 4. **29.** 3. **30.** 4. **31.** $\frac{2}{5}$. **32.** 6. **33.** 9. **34.** 7. **35.** 5. **36.** 6. **37.** 6.

Exercise 10. Page 35

1. 30.

2. Son, 10 yr.; father, 50 yr.

3. 78, 13.

4. 80 ft. broken off; 10 ft. standing.

5. 23, 30.

6. 36, 48.

7. 15, 20.

8. 20.

9. 12.

10. 10, 40.

11. 26, 10.

12. 25, 15.

13. 10, 20.

14. 7, 20.

15. 12, 20.

Exercise 11. Page 36

1. Cow, $42; horse, $168.

2. 81.

3. 2.

4. 30, 40.

5. 25, 26, 27.

6. 5, 6, 7, 8, 9.

7. A, 30 yr.; B, 10 yr.

8. Father, 40 yr., son, 10 yr.

9. 40.

10. 10.

11. $40.

12. 9.

Exercise 12. Page 38

1. 15 men; 30 women; 45 children.

2. 50.

3. 16.

4. 7.

5. 35.

6. 24.

7. 24.

8. 20.

9. 970; 1074.

Exercise 13. Page 39

1. 24.

2. A, \$60; B, \$30.

3. \$3 quarters; 6 bills.

4. 14.

5. \$4 quarters; 20 half-dollars.

6. \$7 ten-dollar bills; 21 one-dollar bills.

7. Father, 32 yr.; son, 8 yr.

8. 20.

Exercise 14. Page 40

1. 9 miles.

2. \$60.

3. \$20 lb. at 65 cts.; 60 lb. at 45 cts.

4. 40.

5. 15,000.

6. 15 in.; 21 in.

7. \$2 doz. at 25 cts.; 5 doz. at 20 cts.

8. \$6 quarters, 18 ten-cent pieces.

Exercise 15. Page 49

1. $40c$.
2. $24a$.
3. $39x$.
4. $51y$.
5. $-26a$.
6. $-40x$.
7. $-17b$.
8. $-66z$.
9. $-20m$.
10. $2d$.
11. 0.
12. $-18g$.
13. a^2.
14. $-21x^3$.
15. 0.
16. $3mn$.
17. 0.
18. $-3a^3b^3c^3$.
19. $-9abcd$.
20. 1.
21. 12.
22. 4.
23. -18.
24. 10.

Exercise 16. Page 53

1. $30a^5$.
2. $40a^4b^3$.
3. $63x^2y^2$.
4. $2a^5b^5c^2$.
5. $9a^7b^9c^9$.
6. $-10a^2$.
7. $12ab$.
8. $-a^4b^3$.
9. $10a^5b^5c$.
10. $12x^7y^5z^2$.
11. $105a^7b^5$.
12. $6a^6b^5c^7$.
13. $-12a^5b^5c^5x^5$.
14. $24a^7b^6c^5$.
15. $-42a^6m^5x^7$.
16. $30x^8y^4z^6$.
17. -46.
18. -3.
19. -8.
20. -17.
21. 9.
22. 12.
23. -102.
24. -41.
25. 174.
26. 6.
27. 30.
28. 372.

Exercise 17. Page 57

1. x^2.
2. $3x^2$.
3. -7.
4. -7.
5. $7x^4$.
6. $9x$.
7. $-4a$.
8. $4x^2y^2$.
9. $-9x$.
10. $5x$.
11. $3y^2$.
12. $-4ab^2$.
13. $12xy^4$.
14. $\frac{3x^3y^3}{5}$.
15. $-\frac{3a}{2}$.
16. $-bd$.
17. acd^2.
18. $-\frac{2xy}{3}$.
19. $5ab$.
20. $4mn$.
21. $\frac{yz^3}{3}$.
22. $-17cd$.
23. $2n^2p$.
24. $\frac{3r^2}{p}$.
25. $-13agt$.
26. $\frac{1}{abc}$.
27. $\frac{3}{2xy^2z^3}$.
28. $\frac{2}{mnp}$.
29. $-\frac{a}{3b^2}$.
30. $-\frac{g}{3mt}$.

Exercise 18. Page 60

1. $2a^2 + 2b^2$.
2. $9a^2 - 2a + 6$.
3. 0.
4. $4x + 4y + 4z$.
5. $2b + 2c$.
6. $4a + 4b + 4c$.
7. $3a^2 + 5a - 2$.
8. $8ab + 3ac$.
9. $6x^3$.
10. $5x^2 + 3xy - 2y^2$.
11. $a^2 - 2b^2$.
12. $4a^3 + 6a + 2$.
13. $3m^3 + 7m^2 + 2$.
14. $2x^3 - 2x^2 + 4x + y$.
15. $7x^3 + 7x^2 + 2$.
16. $a^3 + 3a^2b - 5ab^2 - b^3$.
17. $-a^3 - a^2b - 2ab^2 - 2b^3$.
18. $2x^3 + 2x^2y - xy^2 + 6y^3$.

Exercise 19. Page 63

1. $a - b + c$.

2. $2a - 2b + 6c$.

3. $2a + 3y - 8z$.

4. $x + 4y + 5z$.

5. $2ac + 2bc$.

6. $2ab - 3ac + 4bc$.

7. $x^3 + 3x^2 + 2x - 8$.

8. $x^3 - 7x^2 + 4x$.

9. $2b^3 + 18abc - 15c^3$.

10. $2 - x - 2x^2 + 2x^3$.

11. $-3b^3 - 4c^3 + 6abc$.

12. $-x^4 - 2x^3 + 4x^2 - 7x + 5$.

13. $2x + x^2 + x^3 + x^5$.

14. $2b^3 - 4a^2b + 2ab^2$.

15. $2b^4 - 2a^3b^3 - ab^2$.

16. $4x^3 - 3x^2y - 4xy^2 + 7y^3$.

Exercise 20. Page 65

1. c.

2. $y - b$.

3. $x - 3y - 7c$.

4. $7a + 2b - 2$.

5. $2a + x$.

6. $13x - 15y + 13z$.

7. $2a - 2b + 2c$.

8. $5a + b - 4c$.

9. $4x - 5y + 2z$.

10. $3a - b$.

11. $2x + 3y + z$.

12. $-8x + y$.

13. $6z - 2y - z$.

15. $(a + c)x - (a - b)y + (a - c)z$.

16. $(2a + 5c)x - (3a + 4b)y - (6b + 7c)z$.

17. $(ac - an)x - (bm + cn)y + (a + 3c)z$.

18. $(mn - 1)x - (mn + 1)y + (mn + 1)z$.

Exercise 21. Page 68

1. $x^2 + 7x$.

2. $8x^2 - 12xy$.

3. $14xy - 21y^2$.

4. $2ax - 4a^2$.

5. $bx - 3b^2$.

6. $-6a^3 + 9a^2b$.

7. $10x^2z + 15xz^2$.

8. $5a^3b - 25a^2b^2$.

9. $-x^2y^2 + 3xy^3$.

10. $4x^5 - 6x^4$.

11. $4x^2y - 12y^3$.

12. $-x^4 + 3x^2y^2$.

13. $-a^3b^3 + a^5b^2$.

14. $a^4b^2 + a^5$.

15. $4x^5 - 6x^4 + 2x^3$.

16. $5a^3b - 25a^2b^2 - 5ab^3$.

17. $a^5 + 2a^4b + 2a^3b^2$.

18. $a^3b^3 + 2a^2b^4 + 2ab^5$.

19. $8x^3 - 12x^2y - 18xy^2$.

20. $x^2y + 2xy^2 - y^3$.

21. $a^5 + a^4b^2 + a^2b^3$.

22. $x^2y^2 - 2xy^3 + y^4$.

23. $15a^4b^4 - 20a^3b^5 + 5a^5b^3$.

24. $3a^2x^2y^2 - 9a^2xy^4 + 3a^2y^6$.

25. $x^{15}y^2 - x^{13}y^5 - x^6y^{12}$.

26. $4x^5y^3 - 6x^4y^5 + 4x^3y^6$.

27. $a^{10}x^5y^{10} - a^9x^4y^9 - a^8x^3y^8$.

28. $15a^4b^5 - 10a^3b^6 + 25a^5b^4$.

Exercise 22. Page 72

1. $x^2 + 13x + 42$.

2. $x^2 - x - 42$.

3. $x^2 + x - 42$.

4. $x^2 - 13x + 42$.

5. $x^2 + 3x - 40$.

6. $4x^2 + 12x + 9$.

7. $4x^2 - 12x + 9$.

8. $4x^2 - 9$.

9. $-9x^2 + 12x - 4.$

10. $20x^2 - 47x + 21.$

11. $a^2 + ab - 6b^2.$

12. $a^2 - 12ab + 35b^2.$

13. $25x^2 - 30xy + 9y^2.$

14. $x^2 - bx - cx + bc.$

15. $8m^2 - 10mp + 3p^2.$

16. $a^2 + ab - bc - c^2.$

17. $a^4 - a^3b + 2a^2b^2 - ab^3 + b^4.$

18. $x^5 - 3x^4 - x^3 + 16x^2 - 21.$

19. $a^3 - b^3.$

20. $a^3 + b^3.$

21. $2x^4 + 13x^3 - 9x^2 - 50x + 40.$

22. $9x^5 - 7x^3 + 6x^2 - 2x.$

23. $x^5 - 4x^2y^3 + 3xy^4.$

24. $-a^4 + 4a^3b - 7ab^3 - 2b^4.$

25. $-25a^5b^3 + 20a^4b^4 + 12a^3b^5 - 5a^2b^6 - 2ab^7.$

26. $a^4 - 2a^2b^2 + b^4.$

27. $a^2b^2 + 2abcd - a^2c^2 + c^2d^2.$

28. $-2x^5y^3 + x^4y^4 + 10x^3y^5 - 8x^2y^6 - 3xy^7.$

29. $x^4 - 4x^2y^2 + 4xy^3 - y^4.$

30. $3x^4 - 5x^3y - 12x^2y^2 - xy^3 + 3y^4.$

31. $-a^4 + 6a^2b^2 - b^4.$

32. $a^4 - a^3c + ab^2c - b^4 - 2b^2c^2 + ac^3 - c^4.$

33. $a^4 - 16a^2b^2x^2 + 32a^3b^3x^3 - 16a^4b^4x^4.$

34. $6a^4 + 5a^3bx - 10a^2b^2x^2 + 7ab^3x^3 - 2b^4x^4.$

35. $10x^6y^2 + 14x^5y^3 - 48x^4y^4 + 32x^3y^5 - 16x^2y^6.$

Exercise 23. Page 74

1. $2a^2 - a$.

2. $7a^4 - a$.

3. $7x^2 + 1$.

4. $5m^4 - p^2$.

5. $3x^3 - 5x^2$.

6. $-3x^3 + 1$.

7. $2x^2 - 3x$.

8. $-x^2 + 2$.

9. $a + 2c$.

10. $5x - y$.

11. $ax - 1$.

12. $x + xy$.

13. $-3a + 4b - 2c$.

14. $ab - b^4 - a^2b$.

15. $x^2 - 2xy - 3y^2$.

16. $xy - x^2 - y^2$.

17. $-a^2 + ab + b^2$.

18. $-a + 1 - b$.

19. $-1 + xy - x^2y^2$.

20. $x^2 + 2x + 1$.

21. $a - b - c$.

22. $x^3 - x^2y - y^2$.

23. $ab - 2 - 3b^2$.

24. $a^2c^2 + a - c$.

Exercise 24. Page 79

1. $x + 8$.

2. $x - 8$.

3. $x + 8$.

4. $x - 8$.

5. $a + 5$.

6. $3a + 1$.

7. $a + 5$.

8. $-3a - 2$.

9. $x^2 - x + 1$.

10. $x^4 + x^2 + 1$.

11. $1 + ab + a^2b^2$.

12. $x^2 + 3x + 1$.

13. $a - b + c$.

14. $a + b - c$.

15. $x + y - z$.

16. $c^2 + c + 2$.

17. $x - 2y - z$.

18. $x - a$.

19. $a - 2b + 3c$.

20. $a^2 + 5a + 6$.

21. $q^2 + 3q + 2$.

22. $9a^2 + 6ab + 4b^2$.

23. -65.

24. 10.

25. $7a - 45$.

26. $2x^4$.

Exercise 25. Page 80

1. $2a^2$.

2. $-3a^4 + 2a^3b - 2ab^3 + 4b^4$.

3. x.

4. $a^4 + 2a^2b^2 + b^4 - c^4 + 2c^2d^2 - d^4$.

5. $10y^4 + 8y^3 + 6y^2 + 4y + 2$.

6. 0.

7. $2z - 7y$.

8. $a^3 - 3abc + b^3 + c^3$.

9. $4y^2 - 3xy + 2x^2$.

10. $5a^3b - b^4$.

11. $3x^3 - 2x^2 + 1$.

12. $3c^2 + 24c - 12$.

13. $2b^4$.

14. $10 - 16x - 39x^2 + 2x^3 + 15x^4$.

15. $a^4 - ax^3 + x^4$.

16. $(a - b)x^3 + (b + c)x^2 - (c + 1)x$.

17. $(a + b)x^4 - (a - b)x^3 - (c + 2)x$.

18. $(a + 1)x^3 - (b + c)x^2 + (b - c)x$.

Exercise 26. Page 83

1. $m^2 + 2mn + n^2$.
2. $c^2 - 2ac + a^2$.
3. $a^2 + 4ac + 4c^2$
4. $9a^2 - 12ab + 4b^2$.
5. $4a^2 + 12ab + 9b^2$.
6. $a^2 - 6ab + 9b^2$.
7. $4x^2 - 4xy + y^2$.
8. $y^2 - 4xy + 4x^2$.
9. $a^2 + 10ab + 25b^2$.
10. $4a2 - 20ac + 25c^2$.
11. $x^2 - y^2$.
12. $16a^2 - b^2$.
13. $4b^2 - 9c^2$.
14. $x^2 + 10bx + 25b^2$.
15. $y^2 - 4yz + 4z^2$.
16. $y^2 - 9z^2$.
17. $4a^2 - 9b^2$.
18. $4a^2 - 12ab + 9b^2$.
19. $4a^2 + 12ab + 9b^2$.
20. $25x^2 - 9a^2$.

Exercise 27. Page 86

1. $x^2 + 11x + 28$.
2. $x^2 + 4x - 21$.
3. $x^2 - 6x + 8$.
4. $x^2 - 16x + 60$.
5. $x^2 + 3x - 28$.
6. $x^2 - ax - 2a^2$.
7. $x^2 + 2ax - 3a^2$.
8. $a^2 + 6ac + 9c^2$.
9. $a^2 - 2ax - 8x^2$.
10. $a^2 - 7ab + 12b^2$.
11. $a^4 + a^2c - 2c^2$.
12. $x^2 - 20x + 51$.
13. $x^2 + xy - 30y^2$.
14. $9 + 3x - 2x^2$.
15. $5 - 8x - 4x^2$.
16. $a^2 + ab - 6b^2$.

17. $a^4b^4 - 6a^2b^2x^2 + 5x^4$.

18. $a^6b^2 + 4a^4b^4 - 5a^2b^6$.

19. $x^4y^2 - 4x^3y^3 + 3x^2y^4$.

20. $x^4y^2 + 2x^3y^3 + x^2y^4$.

21. $x^2 + (a + b)x + ab$.

22. $x^2 + (a - b)x - ab$.

23. $x^2 - (a - b)x - ab$.

24. $x^2 - (a + b)x + ab$.

25. $x^2 + (2a + 2b)x + 4ab$.

26. $x^2 - (2a - 2b)x - 4ab$.

27. $x^2 + (2a - 2b)x - 4ab$.

28. $x^2 - (2a + 2b)x + 4ab$.

29. $x^2 + 2ax - 3a^2$.

30. $x^2 + ax - 6a^2$.

Exercise 28. Page 88

1. $x + 2$.

2. $x - 2$.

3. $a + 3$.

4. $a - 3$.

5. $c + 5$.

6. $c - 5$.

7. $7x + y$.

8. $7x - y$.

9. $3b + 1$.

10. $3b - 1$.

11. $4x^2 + 5a$.

12. $4x^2 - 5a$.

13. $3x + 5y$.

14. $a + b - c$.

15. $a - b + c$.

16. $a + 2b - c$.

17. $5a - 7b + 1$.

18. $5a - 7b - 1$.

19. $z + x - y$.

20. $z - x + y$.

21. $a - 2b + c$.

22. $x + 3y + z$.

23. $x + 3y - z$.

24. $a + 2b + 2c$.

25. $a + 2b - 2c$.

26. $1 - 3x + 2y$.

Exercise 29. Page 89

1. $1 + x + x^2$.

2. $1 + 2a + 4a^2$.

3. $1 + 3c + 9c^2$.

4. $4a^2 + 2ab + b^2$.

5. $16b^2 + 12bc + 9c^2$.

6. $9x^2 + 6xy + 4y^2$.

7. $x^2y^2 + xyz + z^2$.

8. $a^2b^2 + 2ab + 4$.

9. $25a^2 + 5ab + b^2$.

10. $a^2 + 2ab + 4b^2$.

11. $a^2 + 4a + 16$.

12. $a^6 + 3a^3 + 9$.

13. $a^8 + a^4x^2y^2 + x^4y^4$.

14. $x^{10} + x^5a^3b^3 + a^6b^6$.

15. $9x^2y^2 + 3xyz^4 + z^8$.

16. $x^2y^2z^2 + xyz + 1$.

17. $4a^2b^2c^2 - 6abc + 9$.

18. $1 + 4xyz + 16x^2y^2z^2$.

Exercise 30. Page 90

1. $1 - x + x^2$.

2. $1 - 2a + 4a^2$.

3. $1 - 3c + 9c^2$.

4. $4a^2 - 2ab + b^2$.

5. $16b^2 - 12bc + 9c^2$.

6. $9x^2 - 6xy + 4y^2$.

7. $4x^2 - 10xy + 25y^2$.

8. $x^2y^2 - xyz + z^2$.

9. $a^2b^2 - 2ab + 4$.

10. $25a^2 - 5ab + b^2$.

11. $a^2 - 2ab + 4b^2$.

12. $a^4 - 4a^2 + 16$.

13. $a^6 - 3a^3 + 9$.

14. $4a^4 - 2a^2b + b^2$.

15. $a^8 - a^4x^2y^2 + x^4y^4$.

16. $x^{10} - x^5a^3b^3 + a^6b^6$.

17. $9x^2y^2 - 3xyz^4 + z^8$.

18. $x^2y^2z^2 - xyz + 1$.

19. $4a^2b^2c^2 - 6abc + 9$.

20. $1 - 4xyz + 16x^2y^2z^2$.

21. $1 - 3a^2bc + 9a^4b^2c^2$.

22. $x^3 + x^2y + xy^2 + y^3$.

23. $x^3 - x^2y + xy^2 - y^3$.

24. $x^4 + x^3y + x^2y^2 + xy^3 + y^4$.

25. $x^4 - x^3y + x^2y^2 - xy^3 + y^4$.

26. $x^5 + x^4y + x^3y^2 + x^2y^3 + xy^4 + y^5$.

27. $x^5 - x^4y + x^3y^2 - x^2y^3 + xy^4 - y^5$.

Exercise 31. Page 93

1. $2x(x - 2)$.

2. $3a(a^2 - 2)$.

3. $5a^2b^2(1 - 2ab)$.

4. $xy(3x + 4y)$.

5. $4a^2b^2(2a + b)$.

6. $3a^2(a^2 - 4 - 2a)$.

7. $4x^2(1 - 2x^2 - 3x^3)$.

8. $5(1 - 2x^2y^2 + 3x^2y)$.

9. $7a(a + 2 - 3a^2)$.

10. $3x^2y^2(xy - 2x^2y^2 - 3)$.

Exercise 32. Page 95

1. $(x^2 + 1)(x + 1)$.

2. $(x^2 + 1)(x - 1)$.

3. $(x + y)(x + z)$.

4. $(x - y)(a - b)$.

5. $(a + b)(a - c)$.

6. $(x + 3)(x - b)$.

7. $(x^2 + 2)(2x - 1)$.

8. $(a - b)(a - 3)$.

9. $(2a - c)(3a + b)$.

10. $(xy + c)(ab + c)$.

11. $(a - b - c)(x - y)$.

12. $(a - b - 2c)(a - b)$.

Exercise 33. Page 97

1. $(2 + x)(2 - x)$.

2. $(3 + x)(3 - x)$.

3. $(3a + x)(3a - x)$.

4. $(5 + x)(5 - x)$.

5. $(5x + a)(5x - a)$.

6. $(4a^2 + 11)(4a^2 - 11)$.

7. $(11a^2+4)(11a^2-4)$.

8. $(2ab+cd)(2ab-cd)$.

9. $(1+xy)(1-xy)$.

10. $(9xy+1)(9xy-1)$.

11. $(7ab+2)(7ab-2)$.

12. $(5a^2b^2+3)(5a^2b^2-3)$.

13. $(3a^4b^3+4x^5)(3a^4b^3-4x^5)$.

14. $(12xy+1)(12xy-1)$.

15. $(10x^3yz^2+1)(10x^3yz^2-1)$.

16. $(1+11a^2b^4c^6)(1-11a^2b^4c^6)$.

17. $(5a+8x^3y^3)(5a-8x^3y^3)$.

18. $(4x^8+5y^9)(4x^8-5y^9)$.

19. $90,000$.

20. $22,760$.

21. $732,200$.

22. 400.

23. $28,972$.

24. $14,248,000$.

Exercise 34. Page 98

1. $(x+y+z)(x+y-z)$.

2. $(x-y+z)(x-y-z)$.

3. $(z+x+y)(z-x-y)$.

4. $(z+x-y)(z-x+y)$.

5. $(x+y+2z)(x+y-2z)$.

6. $(2z+x-y)(2z-x+y)$.

7. $(a+2b+c)(a+2b-c)$.

8. $(a-2b+c)(a-2b-c)$.

9. $(c+a-2b)(c-a+2b)$.

10. $(2a+5c+1)(2a+5c-1)$.

11. $(1+2a-5c)(1-2a+5c)$.

12. $(a+3b+4c)(a+3b-4c)$.

13. $(a-5b+3c)(a-5b-3c)$.

14. $(4c+a-5b)(4c-a+5b)$.

15. $(2a+x+y)(2a-x-y)$.

16. $(b+a-2x)(b-a+2x)$.

17. $(2z+x+3y)(2z-x-3y)$.

18. $(3+3a-7b)(3-3a+7b)$.

19. $(4a+2b+5c)(4a-2b-5c)$.

20. $(5c+3a-2x)(4c-3a+2x)$.

21. $(3a+3b-5c)(3a-3b+5c)$.

22. $(4y+a-3c)(4y-a+3c)$.

23. $(7m+p+2q)(7m-p-2q)$.

24. $(6n+d-2c)(6n-d+2c)$.

25. $(x+y+a+b)(x+y-a-b)$.

26. $(x-y+a-b)(x-y-a+b)$.

27. $(2x+3+2a+b)(2x+3-2a-b)$.

28. $(b-c+a-2x)(b-c-a+2x)$.

29. $(3x-y+2a-b)(3x-y-2a+b)$.

30. $(x-3y+a+2b)(x-3y-a-2b)$.

31. $(x+2y+a+3b)(x+2y-a-3b)$.

32. $(x+y+a-z)(x+y-a+z)$.

Exercise 35. Page 101

1. $(2x-y)(4x^2+2xy+y^2)$.

2. $(x-1)(x^2+x+1)$.

3. $(xy-z)(x^2y^2+xyz+z^2)$.

4. $(x-4)(x^2+4x+16)$.

5. $(5a-b)(25a^2+5ab+b^2)$.

6. $(a-7)(a^2+7a+49)$.

7. $(ab-3c)(a^2b^2+3abc+9c^2)$.

8. $(xyz-2)(x^2y^2z^2+2xyz+4)$.

9. $(2ab-3y^2)(4a^2b^2+6aby^2+9y^4)$.

10. $(4x-y^3)(16x^2+4xy^3+y^6)$.

11. $(3a-4c^2)(9a^2+12ac^2+16c^4)$.

12. $(xy-6z)(x^2y^2+6xyz+36z^2)$.

13. $(4x-9y)(16x^2+36xy+81y^2)$.

14. $(3a-8c)(9a^2+24ac+64c^2)$.

15. $(2x^2-5y)(4x^4+10x^2y+25y^2)$.

16. $(4x^2-3y^5)(16x^8+12x^4y^5+9y^{10})$.

17. $(6-2a)(36+12a+4a^2)$.

18. $(7-3y)(49+21y+9y^2)$.

Exercise 36. Page 102

1. $(x+1)(a^2-x+1)$.

2. $(2x+y)(4x^2-2xy+y^2)$.

3. $(x+5)(x^2-5x+25)$.

4. $(4a+3)(16a^2-12a+9)$.

5. $(xy+z)(x^2y^2-xyz+z^2)$.

6. $(a+4)(a^2-4a+16)$.

7. $(2a^2+b)(4a^4-2a^2b+b^2)$.

8. $(x+7)(x^2-7x+49)$.

9. $(2+xyz)(4-2xyz+x^2y^2z^2)$.

10. $(y^3+4x)(y^6-4y^3x+16x^2)$.

11. $(ab+3x)(a^2b^2-3abx+9x^2)$.

12. $(2yz+x^2)(4y^2z^2-2yzx^2+x^4)$.

13. $(y^3+4x^2)(y^6-4y^3x^2+16x^4)$.

14. $(4a^4+x^5)(16a^8-4a^4x^5+x^{10})$.

15. $(3x^5+2a^2)(9x^{10}-6x^5a^2+4a^4)$.

16. $(3x^3+8)(9x^6-24x^3+64)$.

17. $(7+4x)(49-28x+16x^2)$.

18. $(5+3y)(25-15y+9y^2)$.

Exercise 37. Page 104

1. $(2x+y)(2x+y)$.

2. $(x+3y)(x+3y)$.

3. $(x+8)(x+8)$.

4. $(x+5a)(x+5a)$.

5. $(a-8)(a-8)$.

6. $(a-5b)(a-5b)$.

7. $(c-3d)(c-3d)$.

8. $(2x-1)(2x-1)$.

9. $(2a-3b)(2a-3b)$.

10. $(3a-4b)(3a-4b)$.

11. $(x+4y)(x+4y)$.

12. $(x-4y)(x-4y)$.

13. $(2x-5y)(2x-5y)$.

14. $(1+10a)(1+10a)$.

15. $(7a-2)(7a-2)$.

16. $(6a+5b)(6a+5b)$.

17. $(9x-2b)(9x-2b)$.

18. $(mn+7x^2)(mn+7x^2)$.

Exercise 38. Page 107

1. $(a+2)(a+3)$.

2. $(a-2)(a-3)$.

3. $(a+1)(a+5)$.

4. $(a-1)(a-5)$.

5. $(a-1)(a+5)$.

6. $(a+1)(a-5)$.

7. $(c-3)(c-6)$.
8. $(c+3)(c+6)$.
9. $(c-3)(c+6)$.
10. $(c+3)(c-6)$.
11. $(x+2)(x+7)$.
12. $(x-2)(x-7)$.
13. $(x+2)(x-7)$.
14. $(x-4)(x-5)$.
15. $(x+4)(x-5)$.
16. $(x-4)(x+5)$.
17. $(x-3)(x-7)$.
18. $(x+3)(x-7)$.
19. $(x-3)(x+7)$.
20. $(x-7)(x-8)$.
21. $(x+7)(x-8)$.
22. $(x-1)(x-9)$.
23. $(x+3)(x+10)$.
24. $(x-3)(x+10)$.
25. $(x+3)(x-10)$.
26. $(a-2b)(a+3b)$.
27. $(a+2b)(a-3b)$.
28. $(a-b)(a+4b)$.
29. $(a+b)(a-4b)$.
30. $(ax+7)(ax-9)$.
31. $(a-7x)(a+9x)$.
32. $(a-4b)(a-5b)$.
33. $(xy-3z)(xy-16z)$.
34. $(ab+4c)(ab+11c)$.
35. $(x-4y)(x-9y)$.
36. $(x+7y)(x+12y)$.
37. $(ax-6y)(ax-17y)$.
38. $(x+2y)(x-2y)(x^2-5y^2)$.
39. $(a^2x^2-11y^2)(a^2x^2-13y^2)$.
40. $(a^3b^3-11c^2)(a^3b^3-12c^2)$.
41. $(a+4bc)(a-24bc)$.
42. $(a+8bc)(a-12bc)$.
43. $(a+6bc)(a-16bc)$.
44. $(a-3bc)(a+32bc)$.
45. $(a+2bc)(a-48bc)$.
46. $(a+bc)(a+48bc)$.
47. $(x+9yz)(x-27yz)$.
48. $(xy+13z)(xy-14z)$.

Exercise 39. Page 108

1. $a(a^2-7)$.
2. $ab(3ab-2a^2+3b^2)$.

3. $(a-b+1)(a-b)$.

4. $(a+b+1)(a+b-1)$.

5. $(a+2b)(a^2-2ab+4b^2)$.

6. $(x+2y+1)(x-2y)$.

7. $(a-b)(a^2+ab+b^2+1)$.

8. $(a-3b)(a-3b)$.

9. $(x+1)(x-2)$.

10. $(x+1)(x-3)$.

11. $(x-3)(x+7)$.

12. $(a+2)(a-13)$.

13. $(x^2+3)(a+b)$.

14. $(x-3)(x-y)$.

15. $(x-3)(x-4)$.

16. $(a+2b)(a+3b)$.

17. $(x^2+5)(x^2+5)$.

18. $(x-9)(x-9)$.

19. $(x-10)(x-11)$.

20. $(x+8)(x+11)$.

21. $(x-8)(x+11)$.

22. $(x^2+1)(x-1)$.

23. $x^2(3x+1)(3x-1)$.

24. $(1+a-b)(1-a+b)$.

25. $(a+b)(a^2-ab+b^2+1)$.

26. $(m+n)(m-n)(x+y)$.

27. $(x-y+z)(x-y-z)$.

28. $(z+x-y)(z-x+y)$.

29. $(2a^2+3a-1)(2a^2-3a+1)$.

30. $(2x-y)(4x^2+2xy+y^2)$.

31. $x^2(x-3y)$.

32. $(x-3y)(x^2+3xy+9y^2)$.

33. $(x-5)(x+8)$.

34. $(x-2y)(x+5y)$.

35. $(1+4x)(1-4x)$.

36. $a^2(a^2+3b^2)(a^2-3b^2)$.

37. $x(x+y)(x+2y)$.

38. $x^2(x+y)(x+3y)$.

39. $(x-2y^2)(x-2y^2)$.

40. $(4x^2+1)(4x^2+1)$.

41. $a^2(3a+2c)(3a-2c)$.

42. $ab(a+b)(a-2b)$.

43. $(x+2)(x^2-2x+4)(x-1)$.

44. $(a+y)(a^2-ay+y^2)(a-x)$.

Exercise 40. Page 112

1. 6.
2. $5x^3$.
3. $6ax$.
4. $7ab^2$.
5. 7.
6. $2a^2b^2$.
7. $x + 3y$.
8. $x + 3$.
9. $2a + 1$.
10. $x + y$.
11. $a + x$.
12. $a + 2b$.
13. $x - 1$.
14. $x + 3$.
15. $x - 6$.
16. $x^2 - x + 1$.
17. $x - 1$.
18. $x - y$.
19. $x - 5$.
20. $a - b - c$.
21. $x + 2y$.
22. $x + 4y$.
23. $x^2 + 2xy + 4y^2$.
24. $x - 2$.
25. $1 - 3a$.
26. $x - 7y$.
27. $2a + b$.
28. $x + y - z$.

Exercise 41. Page 115

1. $18x^2y^3$.
2. $6a^2bc^3$.
3. $20a^3b^3$.
4. $30a^3b^4$.
5. $189x^3y^5$.
6. $x^2y^3z^3$.
7. $a^2(a + 1)$.
8. $x^2(x - 3)$.
9. $x(x + 1)(x - 1)$.
10. $x(x + 1)(x - 1)$.
11. $xy(x + y)$.
12. $x(x + 2)^2$.
13. $(a + 2)(a + 2)(a + 3)$.
14. $(c - 4)(c + 5)(c - 6)$.
15. $(b - 5)(b - 6)(b + 7)$.
16. $(y - 4)(y + 5)(y - 6)$.
17. $(z - 5)(z - 6)(z + 7)$.

18. $(x-4)(x+8)(x-8)(x^2+4x+16)$.

19. $(a+b)(a+b)(a-b)(a-b)$.

20. $4a^2b(a+b)(a+b)(a-b)$.

21. $(y+2)(y+3)(y+4)$.

22. $(x+1)(x-1)(x^2+1)$.

23. $(1+x)(1-x)(1+x+x^2)$.

24. $(x+y)(x+y)(x-y)(x-y)$.

25. $x(x-3)(x+5)(x^2+3x+9)$.

26. $(a+b+c)(a+b+c)(a+b-c)$.

27. $(x-a)(x-b)(x-c)$.

28. $a(a+b+c)(a+b-c)$.

Exercise 42. Page 118

1. $\frac{1}{3b}$.

2. $\frac{4m}{5n}$.

3. $\frac{3m}{4p^2}$.

4. $\frac{x^2}{2yz}$.

5. $\frac{a^3b^3}{3c^2}$.

6. $\frac{2xy}{3}$.

7. $\frac{2m}{3p}$.

8. $\frac{3b^2c}{4a^3}$.

9. $\frac{2y^2z^4}{3}$.

10. $\frac{b}{c}$.

11. $\frac{2a-3b}{2a}$.

12. $\frac{3a}{a+2}$.

13. $\frac{x}{x-1}$.

14. $\frac{y}{x^2+3xy+9y^2}$.

15. $\frac{x+1}{x-5}$.

16. $\frac{x+1}{x-2}$.

17. $\frac{a+b+c}{a}$.

18. $\frac{x+5}{x+3}$.

19. $\frac{x+1}{x+3}$.

Exercise 43. Page 120

1. $a+b+\frac{2}{a-b}$.

2. $a-b-\frac{2}{a+b}$.

3. $a-1+\frac{2a}{a^2-a-1}$.

4. $2x-4+\frac{5}{x+1}$.

5. $4x^2-2x+1-\frac{1}{2x+1}$.

6. $5x+4+\frac{x+7}{x^2+x-1}$.

7. $a + \frac{5a-2}{a^2+a+2}$.

8. $y^2 - yx + x^2$.

9. $x^2 - 4x + 3 + \frac{2x-4}{x^2+x+1}$.

10. $x^3 + x + 1 + \frac{2x+2}{x^2-x-1}$.

Exercise 44. Page 122

1. $\frac{x^2+y^2}{x-y}$.

2. $\frac{x^2+y^2}{x+y}$.

3. $\frac{2y}{x+y}$.

4. $-\frac{2ax}{a-x}$.

5. $-\frac{x+2}{x-3}$.

6. $-\frac{2x^2-6x+5}{x-2}$.

7. $\frac{x^3+x^2-2x+1}{x+2}$.

8. $\frac{2a^2-11a+6}{a-3}$.

9. $\frac{-2a^3+a^2+2a-3}{a-1}$.

10. $\frac{3a^4+6a^3-14a^2-4}{3a^2+1}$.

Exercise 45. Page 124

1. $\frac{x(x+a)}{(x+a)(x-a)}, \frac{x^2}{(x+a)(x-a)}$.

2. $\frac{a(a-b)}{(a+b)(a-b)}, \frac{a^2}{(a+b)(a-b)}$.

3. $\frac{1-2a}{(1+2a)(1-2a)}, \frac{1}{(1+2a)(1-2a)}$.

4. $\frac{9}{(4+x)(4-x)}, \frac{(4-x)^2}{(4+x)(4-x)}$.

5. $\dfrac{a^2}{(3-a)(9+3a+a^2)}, \dfrac{a(9+3a+a^2)}{(3-a)(9+3a+a^2)}.$

6. $\dfrac{x+2}{(x+2)(x-2)(x-3)}, \dfrac{x-2}{(x+2)(x-2)(x-3)}.$

Exercise 46. Page 125

1. $\dfrac{4x+2}{5}.$

2. $\dfrac{13x+3}{12}.$

3. $\dfrac{5(9x-13)}{42}.$

4. $\dfrac{51x+31}{36}.$

5. $\dfrac{x-5}{3}.$

6. $\dfrac{5(x-y)}{8x}.$

7. $\dfrac{22x-97}{30}.$

8. $\dfrac{3x-4}{15x}.$

9. $\dfrac{a^3-b^3+c^3-abc}{abc}.$

Exercise 47. Page 127

1. $\dfrac{2x+1}{(x+3)(x-2)}.$

2. $\dfrac{2x}{x^2-1}.$

3. $\dfrac{3x+16}{(x-8)(x+2)}.$

4. $\dfrac{4ax}{a^3-x^2}.$

5. $\dfrac{ax}{x^2-a^2}.$

6. $-\dfrac{4ab}{4a^2-b^2}.$

7. $\dfrac{1}{9-a^2}.$

8. $\dfrac{b}{a^2-b^2}.$

9. $\dfrac{5x+8}{x^2-4}.$

10. $\dfrac{1+x}{1-9x^2}.$

11. $\dfrac{3(a^2+4a+1)}{a(a+1)(a+3)}.$

12. $\dfrac{2}{x^2-1}.$

13. $\dfrac{2x^2}{(x+2)(x-3)}.$

14. 0.

Exercise 48. Page 128

1. 0.

2. $\dfrac{2a}{a+b}.$

3. $\dfrac{7a}{1-a^2}.$

4. $\dfrac{x-10y}{4x^2-25y^2}.$

5. $\dfrac{2}{x+4y}.$

6. $\dfrac{2(x+6)}{4x^2-9}.$

Exercise 49. Page 131

1. $\frac{20}{3bc}$.
2. $\frac{2ay}{3}$.
3. $\frac{7p^2}{4xz}$.
4. $\frac{2a^2cm}{7}$.
5. $\frac{30}{abc}$.
6. abc.
7. b^2.
8. $\frac{x+a}{x-2a}$.
9. $\frac{xy}{2c-1}$.
10. $\frac{a+10}{a+3}$.
11. $\frac{3x+2y}{x-2}$.
12. $\frac{5a+b}{4a+3b}$.
13. $\frac{x-7}{a+b+c}$.
14. $\frac{x(x+1)}{x-5}$.
15. $\frac{a+1}{a+5}$.
16. 1.
17. $\frac{x(x+y)}{x+1}$.
18. $\frac{b}{a-b}$.
19. abc.
20. $\frac{(x+2y)(x+1)}{(x+y)(x+2)}$.

Exercise 50. Page 134

1. $\frac{x+y}{z}$.
2. $\frac{12x+3y}{12x-4y}$.
3. $\frac{abd-21d^2}{21cd-7ab}$.
4. $\frac{x^2+x-2}{x^2-x-2}$.
5. 1.
6. $\frac{x+y}{x^2-2xy+y^2}$.
7. $\frac{a+b}{a-b}$.
8. $4(3a+8)$.
9. $\frac{y+x}{y-x}$.
10. x.
11. $\frac{1}{x}$.
12. $\frac{x^2(x-3)}{x-2}$.
13. $a-1$.
14. $\frac{4a}{a-x}$.

Exercise 51. Page 139

1. 5. **2.** 7. **3.** $2\frac{1}{2}$. **4.** 120. **5.** 12.

6. $2\frac{1}{3}$. **7.** 17. **8.** 4. **9.** 4. **10.** 1. **11.** -16. **12.** 11. **13.** -4. **14.** -2. **15.** -2. **16.** 5. **17.** 9. **18.** -1.

Exercise 52. Page 140

1. 2. **2.** 2. **3.** -33. **4.** 1. **5.** $\frac{2}{3}$. **6.** $1\frac{1}{2}$. **7.** 2. **8.** 8. **9.** 5. **10.** $\frac{3}{7}$. **11.** 2. **12.** 1. **13.** 3.

Exercise 53. Page 142

1. 33. **2.** 2. **3.** $3\frac{1}{2}$. **4.** $1\frac{5}{37}$. **5.** 7. **6.** 3.

Exercise 54. Page 143

1. $a+b$. **2.** $\frac{a}{2}$. **3.** $\frac{b}{2}$. **4.** $2a$. **5.** $b-a$. **6.** $\frac{ab}{a+b+c}$. **7.** $\frac{a^2-b^2}{2a}$. **8.** $\frac{2b}{a}$. **9.** $\frac{2b^2-a^2}{4b-3a}$. **10.** 1. **11.** $3(a-b)$.

Exercise 55. Page 144

1. 35. **2.** 70. **3.** 36. **4.** 57, 58.

Exercise 56. Page 145

1. 81, 19. **2.** 100, 24. **3.** 64, 15. **4.** 103, 12. **5.** 295, 25.

Exercise 57. Page 147

1. 12 yr.
2. A, 60 yr.; B, 10 yr.
3. A, 25 yr.; B, 5 yr.
4. $17\frac{1}{2}$ yr.
5. 35 yr.
6. Son, 12 yr.; father, 36 yr.
7. 25 yr.
8. A, 30 yr.; B, 15 yr.
9. Son, 12 yr.; father, 68 yr.

Exercise 58. Page 148

1. $1\frac{3}{7}$ dy. **2.** $1\frac{13}{47}$ dy. **3.** $1\frac{1}{20}$ dy. **4.** 15 dy. **5.** 12 hr. **6.** 10 dy.

Exercise 59. Page 150

1. $7\frac{5}{13}$ hr. **2.** $2\frac{2}{5}$ hr. **3.** $\frac{10}{11}$ hr. **4.** $1\frac{1}{13}$ hr. **5.** 30 hr.

Exercise 60. Page 151

1. 36 mi. **2.** 26 hr. **3.** 8 mi. **4.** 240 mi.

Exercise 61. Page 152

1. 600. **2.** 700. **3.** Dog, 1440; rabbit, 1800.

Exercise 62. Page 154

1. $27\frac{3}{11}$ min. past 5 o'clock. **2.** $27\frac{3}{11}$ min. past 2 o'clock.

3. $43\frac{7}{11}$ min. past 2 o'clock.

4. $21\frac{9}{11}$ min. past 1 o'clock.

5. $38\frac{2}{11}$ min. past 1 o'clock.

6. $38\frac{2}{11}$ min. past 7 o'clock.

Exercise 63. Page 155

1. 1764 sq. ft.

2. 18 ft. by 23 ft.

3. 14 ft. by 20 ft.

4. 12 ft. by 15 ft.

5. 30 ft. by 40 ft.

Exercise 64. Page 160

1. $90° 0' 30''$; $30° 30'$.

2. $\$133\frac{1}{3}$.

3. \$2000.

4. \$4000.

5. \$3000.

6. \$500.

7. 5%.

8. 6%.

9. 3 yr.

10. $9\frac{3}{8}$ yr.

11. \$25,000.

12. \$20,000.

13. \$6%.

14. 20 yr.

Exercise 65. Page 165

1. $x = 2$, $y = 1$.

2. $x = 3$, $y = 2$.

3. $x = 5$, $y = 1$.

4. $x = 2$, $y = 1$.

5. $x = 1$, $y = 2$.

6. $x = 6$, $y = 1$.

7. $x = 3$, $y = 21$.

8. $x = 7$, $y = 7$.

9. $x = 23$, $y = -1$.

10. $x = 2$, $y = 1$.

11. $x = 35$, $y = 20$.

12. $x = 2$, $y = 1$.

13. $x = 1$, $y = 2$.

14. $x = 3$, $y = 2$.

15. $x = 1$, $y = 2$.

16. $x = 4$, $y = 3$.

17. $x = 12$, $y = 4$.

18. $x = 12$, $y = 21$.

19. $x = 5$, $y = 7$.

20. $x = 5$, $y = 2$.

21. $x = 18$, $y = 6$.

22. $x = 3$, $y = 2$.

23. $x = 3$, $y = 2$.

24. $x = 7$, $y = 8$.

25. $x = 8$, $y = -2$.

26. $x = \frac{a}{(a-b)}$, $y = \frac{b}{(a+b)}$.

Exercise 66. Page 168

1. A, \$520; B, \$440.

2. 23 and 17.

3. 20 and 16.

4. Velvet, \$6; silk, \$3.

5. Wheat, \$1; rye, $\$\frac{4}{5}$.

6. Tea, $\$\frac{1}{2}$; coffee, $\$\frac{1}{4}$.

7. Horse, \$92; cow, \$64.

Exercise 67. Page 169

1. $\frac{3}{7}$. **2.** $\frac{13}{25}$. **3.** $\frac{3}{20}$. **4.** $\frac{5}{21}$. **5.** $\frac{7}{22}$.

Exercise 68. Page 171

1. 45. **2.** 72. **3.** 75 and 57. **4.** 54.

Exercise 69. Page 172

1. \$2500 at 4%. **2.** \$1600 at 6%. **3.** \$6000 at 4%; \$4000 at 5%.

Exercise 70. Page 173

1. 22 and 18.

2. 60 and 8.

3. $\frac{14}{17}$.

4. Wheat, \$1; barley, $\$\frac{4}{5}$.

5. A, \$235; B, \$65.

6. A, \$70; B, \$30.

7. Lemon, 2 cts.; orange, 3 cts.

8. A, 30 apples; B, 10 apples.

Exercise 71. Page 178

1. ± 2. **2.** ± 3. **3.** ± 5. **4.** ± 8.

5. ± 7.

6. ± 5.

7. ± 5.

8. ± 3.

9. ± 3.

10. ± 3.

11. 12 and 16.

12. 12 oranges at 3 cts.

13. 3 rods.

14. Width, 12 rd.; length, 48 rd.

Exercise 72. Page 181

1. 9 or 3.

2. 4 or 2.

3. 3 or 1.

4. 1 or $-\frac{1}{5}$.

5. 1 or -3.

6. $\frac{4}{3}$ or $\frac{4}{3}$.

7. 1 or $-\frac{1}{6}$.

8. 3 or -1.

9. $\frac{3}{4}$ or $\frac{1}{4}$.

10. 3 or $\frac{1}{3}$.

11. 17 or -3.

12. 25 or 9.

13. 4 or -5.

14. 4 or -3.

15. 5 or 1.

16. 2 or -6.

17. 2 or 2.

18. 5 or -11.

19. 2 or $-5\frac{1}{3}$.

20. $4\frac{1}{3}$ or $-3\frac{2}{3}$.

21. 2 or $\frac{1}{3}$.

22. 4 or $-\frac{2}{5}$.

23. 2 or -3.

24. 10 or 2.

25. 3 or $-2\frac{1}{3}$.

26. 2 or 2.

27. $\frac{1}{2}$ or -3.

28. 5 or $\frac{1}{2}$.

29. 7 or 2.

30. 4 or $-\frac{2}{3}$.

31. 8 or 2.

32. 4 or -7.

33. 0 or 3.

34. 0 or 7.

35. 5 or 2.

36. 4 or -1.

Exercise 73. Page 186

1. 6 and 5.

2. 5 and 15.

3. Son, 8 yr.; father, 40 yr.

4. 9.

6. 5 rd. by 7 rd.

7. 12 ft.
8. 20 ft. by 18 ft.
9. 10 rd. by 12 rd.
10. Son, 10 yr.; father, 54 yr.

Exercise 74. Page 187

1. 6 miles an hour.
2. 7.
3. 5.
4. 8.
5. 36.

Exercise 75. Page 192

1. 75.
2. 38.
3. $4\frac{1}{7}$.
4. $-8\frac{3}{4}$.
5. 23.
6. 0.
7. 156.
8. 20th.
9. 101st.
10. 26.
11. a.
12. 21, 22, etc.

Exercise 76. Page 195

1. 440.
2. 201.
3. $4frac16$.
4. 128.
5. -378.
6. $187\frac{1}{2}$.
7. 1, 3, 5.
8. 156.
9. 300.
10. 2550 yd.
11. 5812.1 ft.
12. 144.9 ft.
13. 11, 15.
14. 7, 9, 11.
15. 12 miles.
16. 5, 12, 19.

Exercise 77. Page 201

1. 243.
2. 192.
3. $\frac{3}{64}$.
4. 256.
5. ± 4.
6. ± 4.
7. 1092.
8. 765.
9. $11\frac{29}{32}$.
10. $15\frac{15}{16}$.
11. $127\frac{3}{4}$.
12. 44.
13. $1\frac{11}{54}$.
14. $1.27.
15. $81.90.
16. $14,641$.

Exercise 78. Page 205

1. $a + b + c$.
2. $x^2 + x + 1$.
3. $x^2 - 2xy + y^2$.
4. $2a^2 - 3ab + 5b^2$.
5. $4x^3 + 3x^2y - 2y^3$.
6. $2x^3 - xy^2 + 3y^3$.

Exercise 79. Page 210

1. 18.
2. 21.
3. 23.
4. 31.
5. 3.2.
6. 7.3.
7. 232.
8. 785.
9. 1225.
10. 589.
11. 5601.
12. 1234.
13. 1.4142...
14. 1.7320...
15. 2.2360...
16. 2.4494...
17. 0.7071...
18. 0.9486...
19. 0.8164...
20. 0.8660...
21. 0.8944...
22. 0.7905...

Exercise 80. Page 213

1. $x + y$.
2. $2x - 1$.
3. $2x - 3y$.
4. $4a - 3x$.
5. $1 + x + x^2$.
6. $x^2 - x + 1$.

Exercise 81. Page 219

1. 36.
2. 35.
3. 45.
4. 65.
5. 48.
6. 637.
7. 478.
8. 638.
9. 503.
10. 728.
11. 12.34.
12. 12.25.
13. 0.2154...
14. 0.3684...
15. 0.5848...
16. 1.5874...
17. 2.1544...
18. 4.4310...
19. 1.3572...
20. 1.2703...
21. 1.4454...
22. 0.8735...
23. 0.9085...
24. 0.9352...